# A Guide to Evaluation
## for Arts Therapists
## and Arts & Health Practitioners

# A Guide to Evaluation

## for Arts Therapists and Arts & Health Practitioners

*Giorgos Tsiris,
Mercédès Pavlicevic
and Camilla Farrant*

*Foreword by Mike White*

Jessica Kingsley *Publishers*
London and Philadelphia

First published in 2014
by Jessica Kingsley Publishers
73 Collier Street
London N1 9BE, UK
and
400 Market Street, Suite 400
Philadelphia, PA 19106, USA

*www.jkp.com*

**Library of Congress Cataloging in Publication Data**
Tsiris, Giorgos.
   A guide to evaluation for arts therapists and arts & health practitioners / Giorgos Tsiris,
Mercédès Pavlicevic and Camilla Farrant ; foreword by Mike White.
      pages cm
   Includes bibliographical references and index.
   ISBN 978-1-84905-418-8 (alk. paper)
   1. Arts--Therapeutic use. 2. Art therapists. 3. Psychotherapy. 4. Clinical psychology--
Practice--Evaluation. I. Pavlicevic, Mercédès II. Farrant, Camilla. III. Title.
   RC489.A7T77 2013
   616.89'1656--dc23

                         2013032696

**British Library Cataloguing in Publication Data**
A CIP catalogue record for this book is available from the British Library

ISBN 978 1 84905 418 8
eISBN 978 0 85700 800 8

Printed and bound in Great Britain

# Contents

# Figures and Tables

# Foreword

In my previous life as a local government arts officer, I was once asked by an internal auditor why I had for two years consecutively booked the same clown to provide children's entertainment in branch libraries. Had I tested the market and assessed the cost value of the work? Calmly incredulous, I replied that I had made a subjective judgement that this clown was funnier than the other clowns, coupled with an objective observation that his make-up did not scare the smaller children, and that I had also, through a process review, determined that his magic tricks were transparent but effective. I admit this was not a wholly evidence-based response, but it was aimed as a satirical barb at a common misconception of evaluation as a reductionist correlation of cost and value irrespective of context.

Unfortunately, that blinkered thinking still applies in the health sector's peremptory challenge to the arts to prove their worth in delivering individual health and social wellbeing – as if human flourishing were not the mission and core business of the arts from time immemorial. In recent years, the field of arts in health has had an influx of interdisciplinary theorists, cultural ideologists and empiricist evaluators jostling for position in an emergent research community. Positions have sometimes become entrenched and then it seems more like a dysfunctional family squabbling over the hypothetical inheritance that may come when commissioners and policy makers accept an evidence base for the benefits of arts in health.

So it is a relief to have here a practical guide to DIY evaluation of arts in health[1] that does exactly what it says on the tin. By clearly focusing on value in context and reflexivity in practice to determine its meaning, we are offered appropriate evaluation tools that work from the inside out. It sensibly distinguishes between evaluation and research, and by being context-specific rather than practice-specific in assessing the utility of its methodologies, it offers entry points for practitioners from a wide range of backgrounds. In 25 years of assisting the development of this work, it has become clear to me that arts in health is not delivered by the artist or therapist in isolation, but rather through a confluence of inter-professional interests and disciplines. In this increasingly diverse field of art in health, art therapists lead on the application of supervision and reflective practice to their work, and other arts practitioners should do likewise because guided reflection is a natural pause in creativity and is the soul-mate of evaluation.

The combined research agenda of arts in healthcare settings, health promotion and therapies is now vast, as there is a broad spectrum of practice which is still innovative and curious. We must not stifle its emergent vision and potential by only seeking a proven evidence base that is narrowly defined through the 'gold standard' of control-based interventions; that reduces the whole arts and health field to being some kind of ancillary treatment. To adapt an aphorism of Oscar Wilde, there seems little point in knowing the price of arts interventions in a medical model of healthcare if we do not also appreciate their value in addressing inequalities through social models of preventative or restorative healthcare. We are not interested only in cause and effect with a few variables; rather we thrive on the complexity of intractably difficult things to explain beyond phenomenology. It is inherent

---

1    Authors' note: There is a subtle (and at times fuzzy) distinction between arts *in* health, and arts *and* health throughout the Foreword, which may puzzle readers outside the UK. The former generally refers to arts practices in community or care, while arts *and* health designates an emerging field of practices (and practitioners) that includes community artists, arts therapists and 'arts & health' practitioners.

in the effectiveness of arts interventions in health that it is permitted, within safe and supportive parameters, to engage with the 'madness' of art and its making. By its very nature, art pushes against barriers, boundaries and preconceptions, and its creative energy in promoting health may necessarily be volatile. This is why qualitative evidence from participants repeatedly affirms the felt experience through art as a counter to the circumstances and symptoms of ill health or social exclusion.

Some evaluations focus specifically on arts and health and look for evidence of therapeutic benefit, whilst others take a broader perspective in attempting to identify a connection between cultural participation and wellbeing and how that impacts on both individuals and their communities. Both approaches are valid but fraught with problems, so it seems important first to establish what practitioners hope to achieve from their activities. This publication is timely because many are now attempting to evaluate, but they are struggling to find appropriate methods. A serious and widespread shortcoming is a failure to state and agree clear aims for a project. There is uncertainty about what evaluation methods to use and what methods will be acceptable to other stakeholders. There is also concern that a requirement for quantitative evaluation will affect and damage the delivery of the work. In particular there is concern about the requirements of medical practice. Whatever method of evaluation is adopted, practitioners can only collect appropriate data and evidence if they are clear about their aims, and about what effect is intended.

Before embarking on more refined experimental approaches, it needs to be recognised that there are crucial misunderstandings around the aims, intentions and evidence for art and health activity, and there seems to be a mismatch between the aims of the practitioners and the expectations of those requesting the evidence. In order to make progress in this search for evidence, it is essential that all parties clarify their intentions, assumptions and requirements. The practitioners need to state clearly what they are aiming to achieve. The funders and others who request evidence need to state clearly for what effects they require it, and what would be acceptable as evidence. The underlying dilemma, of course, is that unless the arts in health field produces a more rigorous evidence base for its work, it will not gain access to better sources of funding from the health sector, and because it does not have access to sufficient funding, it is struggling to work up this evidence base. If together arts in health practitioners and art therapists could concur on some common aims and issues, agree ways of evaluating them with the help of this guide, and then share and collate the results, the field could achieve a critical mass of information.

This guide usefully offers different means of testing and explaining the effects of participatory arts on health improvement. The arts sector is open perhaps to making catholic interpretations based on processes of creative engagement, but medical science seems less ready to accept holistic forms of explanation for the presentation of individual pathology. Because crucial decisions have to be made on that presentation, success is predicated on short-term beneficial treatment of individuals rather than the complex evolution of a social cure. Arts in health tended in the past to waver between the two in attempting to prove its efficacy. In the field of medical humanities, however, the 'interpretivist' approach is having a growing influence on clinicians in their patient consultations. It is not only a means of evaluation, but a medium for ascertaining a diagnosis that connects individuals' illnesses with their whole selves and social circumstances – and this is where I feel arts in health practitioners and arts therapists could really contribute through complementary practices. The psychological dimension of narrative-based medicine brings a contextual relevance to the identification of symptoms and appropriate treatment, but this can also highlight the need for recovery pathways through social reintegration and cultural engagement. If health might be conceived in the psychological domain as a search for meaning, then reflective practice and art's search for value can be important adjuncts in the production of these pathways.

The emergence of small cross-national collaborations in arts in health brings additional significance to qualitative, narrative-based evaluation because of the need to respect and reconcile differing cultural nuances in the application of creativity to health. Finding common ground here precedes the challenge of identifying the relative medical and cost benefits across different systems of health education and welfare. The 'healthy living' stories we generate and exchange are the basis for an international practice and make for fascinating evaluation.

What we should not forget, in doing evaluation, is that arts in health is essentially about relational working, whether it be in acute clinical settings, residential care or a community health context. In looking for impact, we also should not underestimate the inherent strength of the arts to shape people's world view and influence lifestyle choice, autonomy and social engagement – all of which, of course, have significant effects on health. As multi-sector collaborations increasingly assist the delivery of arts in health, and as theoretical disciplines converge to examine its effects, the field is broadening the research agenda around a social model of health. This must not, however, diminish the ability it also has to illuminate and inform the work of medical and health professionals. Investigation into therapeutic effects and the reliable attribution of benefit for healthcare from the arts should continue and be properly examined and compared in both participatory arts and arts therapy contexts. There is otherwise a danger of over-generalising health gain from social capital outcomes. In the UK, the recent transfer of the public health function out of NHS primary care services and into local government presents additional challenges for the orientation of arts in health evaluations.

In future, what could help maintain a balance between sociological and clinical investigation would be a closer alliance between the diverse practice of the arts in health field, the professional discipline of arts therapies and the sharpening vision of medical humanities. Such an alliance could help overcome many of the difficulties and dilemmas that have so far hampered the development of a credible evidence base for the effectiveness of participatory arts in health. In a community of interest driven by passionate practice and a cooperative spirit of inquiry, evaluation will come naturally if we remember it is only as complex as life itself – and there's the rub.

*Mike White*
*Centre for Medical Humanities, Durham University*

# Acknowledgments

We would like to thank the many Nordoff Robbins music therapists who have collaborated with us over the years in designing and conducting monitoring and evaluation projects on their work in a range of settings across the UK.

Much of the material presented in the guide has been refined and developed in our evaluation training courses with arts therapy and arts & health practitioners and students: we are grateful for their astute comments and awkward questions.

A warm thanks goes to Mike White for his passionate commitment to developing substantial critical thinking to the field of arts & health across the globe; and thanks also to Mike and to Tom Smith for permission to use the 'Key Dimensions' diagram.

We would like to thank the Nordoff Robbins Communications Department and Nicky O'Neill for giving us permission for the use of photographs and pictures distributed throughout this guide.

Finally, we thank our colleagues Neta Spiro and Tamar File, in the Nordoff Robbins Research Department, for their constant support and insightful comments throughout the writing process of this guide.

# Introduction

'axiologisi' (Greek): 'axia' (value) + 'logos' (speech/reason)

'évaluer' (French): 'é-' (from) + 'valuer' (to value)

'Life is difficult!'

'…in relation to what?'

*Groucho Marx*

Evaluation is part of everyday life. We consider, compare, revise our reference frames and make decisions on the basis of – at times subliminal – sifting of information and weighing up of ongoing accumulation of experiences: what is more or less, what is different (from what); what is different this time round (and why, how and who says so); does something work better before or after; what seems better value for our money; which of several dwellings might better suit our purposes…and more.

Evaluation – whether implicit or explicit, informal or structured – is part of everyday work. Many organisations that employ arts & health and arts therapy practitioners have or require specialist evaluation procedures, to ensure fit-for-purpose services, activities, systems or products. Some organisations prefer to use external evaluators, who are more or less familiar with arts & health practices and with organisation-specific values and ethos.

A conundrum emerges. How stable are values, across arts-based practices, services, worksites and sectors? Which values, and whose, hold weight and why might this be? 'How do evaluation procedures resonate with disparate and at times irreconcilable values?'

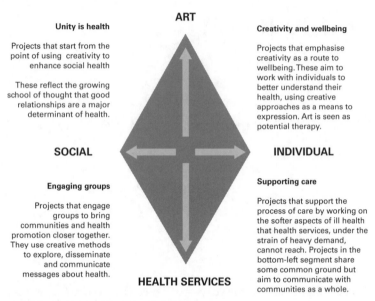

**ART**

**Unity is health**

Projects that start from the point of using creativity to enhance social health

These reflect the growing school of thought that good relationships are a major determinant of health.

**Creativity and wellbeing**

Projects that emphasise creativity as a route to wellbeing. These aim to work with individuals to better understand their health, using creative approaches as a means to expression. Art is seen as potential therapy.

**SOCIAL**          **INDIVIDUAL**

**Engaging groups**

Projects that engage groups to bring communities and health promotion closer together. They use creative methods to explore, disseminate and communicate messages about health.

**Supporting care**

Projects that support the process of care by working on the softer aspects of ill health that health services, under the strain of heavy demand, cannot reach. Projects in the bottom-left segment share some common ground but aim to communicate with communities as a whole.

**HEALTH SERVICES**

FIGURE 1 KEY DIMENSIONS OF ARTS/HEALTH
Source: White, 2009, p.92

Mike White (2009) and Tom Smith (2003) present the multifaceted orientations of arts & health philosophies and practices through a diamond (Figure 1); a fitting symbol for stability and movement. For example, arts practices at the tip of the top arrow emphasise creativity, flexibility, imagination, while the health services at the bottom may well be straining towards understandings of health, situated within the individual (bottom right quadrant). Since there are sure to be infinite variations within and between quadrants and arrows, how might the values signalled by both the distinctive and the linked dimensions engage with one another in an evaluation? What value might there be in retaining irreconcilable values?

This book suggests that the practitioner's evaluation skill may well be to synthesise and maintain such polarities in ways that manage to also insist on retaining arts-based values.

Evaluation empowers:[2] a respectful invitation and listening to people voicing opinions, complaints and suggestions on the basis of their arts-based participative experiences. Since evaluation is part of professional accountability and integrity, this guide's uncompromising stance is that, however complicated their planning and procedures, robust and systematic evaluations are core to ethical, imaginative and fitting delivery of arts-based practices.

While the link between arts & health work and arts therapy work is often portrayed as tenuous (and at times polarised), our experiences of evaluation training workshops with arts therapists and arts & health practitioners reveal more similarities than differences between them. All are arts-based, many engage similar populations in the same settings, and any of these practices, in whatever site or sector, face the same conundrums: of assessing and conveying arts-based values in contexts that privilege quantity and generalisable (outcome) measures. This guide signals this inclusive understanding through using more generic professional terms (e.g. services, practitioners, arts-based practices) throughout.

As three music therapy practitioners, researchers and evaluators based within Nordoff Robbins Music Therapy (the UK's largest music therapy charity), this guide's evaluation toolkit offers a blueprint assembled from evaluations we have completed on a range of practices in a range of settings (health, education, social care, community). These evaluations take into account the values held by practitioners, service users, their families, as well as staff members, managers and funders, which is not always a comfortable fit!

This guide contends that practitioners have no option but to evaluate and is designed to help those associated with arts & health and arts therapy practices to be proactive rather than reactive in terms of evaluating their services within the workplace. It is addressed, in the first instance, to practitioners, but also to

----

2   Music therapists Simon Procter and Randi Rolvsjord draw from Empowerment philosophy to question sociocultural tendencies to minimise the musical, cultural and social resources of mental health clients (in particular) (Procter, 2002; Rolvsjord, 2004).

researchers, students, employers and managers who may be considering how best to ensure that fit-for-purpose, systematic evaluation procedures ensure effective delivery of services.

Two caveats: this guide is not concerned with *practice-specific* value evaluations or assessments (e.g. music therapy assessment scales that assess clients' therapeutic developments over time); in other words, it is not concerned with assigning practice-specific value through more introspective, practice-based procedures. It focuses instead on an external, organisational view of arts-based services, using evaluation criteria that relate closely to (or are specific to) their organisational contexts, while also attending to the specificities of arts-based health practices. The second caveat concerns the inevitable local–global tensions around evaluation norms, discourses and values. From trawling within and across localities and nations, we hope to present essential, foundational information and guidance for practitioners, while also encouraging practitioners to adapt or design fit-for-purpose evaluation tools for arts-based services and projects.

In addition to encouraging practitioners to 'do it for themselves', this guide alerts practitioners to the pitfalls and possibilities of 'external' evaluations of their work. One aim is to help practitioners ensure that external and organisational (and, to reiterate, not practice-specific) evaluation criteria are themselves fit-for-purpose for the services being evaluated. At times, tested evaluation procedures that are considered robust and are routinely used by an organisation may not be the best option for arts-based services. Indeed, these may portray practices in a negative light. Likewise, the contemporary emphasis on proving 'efficacy' and on 'evidence-based' practices often imposes paradigms that do not fit the distinctive nature of arts-based practices and risk, distorting the reporting of their impact (Raw *et al.*, 2012).

Since this guide is not concerned with *researching* arts & health and arts therapy practices, the distinction between research and evaluation needs some comment. Where evaluation is often seen as a poorer cousin of research, carrying less academic and professional status, it has been our experience that data elicited during evaluations has triggered ideas that have inspired research studies. The two, while closely connected, are distinct activities. Where research seeks to develop disciplinary and cross-disciplinary knowledge and theory through a range of research methods and tools, evaluation targets services to assess if, to what extent and how services fulfil their aims and objectives within the workplace. In contrast to evaluations, whose scope tends to be service-specific, research seeks to venture into territories beyond service, professional practice and discipline. While research is subject to research ethics applications procedures, evaluation studies are not necessarily so.[3]

Evaluation, we suggest, needs to weigh evaluation data against the values of the working context. What makes evaluation useful is asking and answering questions about quality and value. For example, it is not just measuring outcomes, but being able to say how substantial, how valuable or how equitable those outcomes are – each of these is an intrinsic value statement. It is not just reporting on whether a service plan was implemented as planned, but saying how well, how effectively or ineffectively, or how appropriate or inappropriate an arts-based implementation has been shown to be (and who says so). It is not just reporting whether the project was delivered within budget, but asking how cost-effective the project was. Evaluations have consequences on service development and funding: informed decisions can be made through addressing the focused and critical questions about value.

This guide conveys our stance, which is acknowledged through the etymology of 'evaluation'. Based on the systematic gathering, ongoing monitoring and robust assessment of information, evaluation examines values and assumptions within the workplace. Information, however well organised and elegantly assembled, remains incomplete without explicitly assigned value. Indeed, we argue that the value of ostensibly 'value-free' evidence is questionable. In this sense, we might posit that evaluation has an element of advocacy and activism to which practitioners need to be alert. We argue equally that the values embedded within evaluation frameworks need to resonate with organisational/

---

3    See Farrant, Pavlicevic and Tsiris (2014).

practice-based values. At times, it is this very resonance that evaluations examine. While evaluation needs to take into account the value-led criteria of an organisation, frameworks informed exclusively by those criteria can be too distant for arts-based practitioners. These understandings suggest that planning an evaluation needs thorough discerning of the distinct and diverse value systems that contribute to the complexities of 'the workplace'.

This guide therefore argues for a stance that acknowledges the complex and – at times colliding – values embedded within arts-based services, the worksites, and within the evaluations. We advocate that data collection and analysis are value-laden, and that all evaluators – whether internal or external, familiar or unfamiliar with arts-based practices – have value-based commitments that shape their designs. It would be unwise to ignore or to sidestep the political agendas (however implicit) that accompany evaluations.

While many arts-based practitioners are familiar with notions of evaluation, fewer are trained to plan, design and follow through such a process or are sufficiently informed to participate in evaluations prompted by internal or external demands. Our first stance, therefore, is that practitioners need to be up to speed with methods, tools and designs, irrespective of whether or not they themselves undertake evaluations – and there are strong arguments for and against DIY evaluations which are mostly circumstantial. This guide provides practitioners with an evaluation toolkit, with pros and cons regarding a range of designs, instruments and outcome measures that are and are not practice-related.

Our second stance is that arts-based practice does not comfortably translate into the values portrayed and conveyed by verbal or numeric signifiers. Music, art, images, dramatic plots and moving arts have distinctive rigours and principles, informed by distinctive epistemological and methodological paradigms. Some of these rigours and principles may be amplified, reduced, distorted and almost certainly changed through numeric or verbal representations. The evaluative act itself risks interrupting, freezing or interfering with the temporality and momentum inherent in the human experiences of shared participatory arts-based practices. These disruptions are rather more complicated than questions of what is gained and lost in translation – and practitioners are invited to minimise the risks of misrepresentation through sustaining a critically curious stance about the complexities of the translation processes.

Weak evaluation designs can result in counterproductive, disempowering endeavours that waste time and precious resources. Like practice, evaluations need to be efficient and effective, designed to fit competently with the (at times) more distant, original agendas and questions that prompt the evaluation.

We aim to support practitioners to be proactive, bold, well informed and resourced regarding evaluation pitfalls and problems, and to be 'equipped' with a range of (at times necessary) avoidance and repair strategies. Since practitioners' effective engagement with data collection and analysis processes is a key factor, not only for the sustainability and expansion of professional practices, but also for ensuring that service users receive the best possible practices, a cautious 'armchair' approach is not an option.

Finally, we aim to inspire practitioners to dare to collect data in ways that that may seem counterintuitive; to complement (and at times challenge) findings from external evaluations (whose criteria may have little to do with the very nature of practices themselves); and to venture boldly well beyond the comforts of 'advocacy'.

## Evaluation phases and the structure of the guide

After the 'Evaluation Basics', which provides basic concepts and values, the guide presents the evaluation process in six phases: (1) planning, (2) developing data collection tools, (3) collecting data and supplementary material, (4) processing data and supplementary material, (5) drafting outputs and (6) finalising and disseminating outputs. As a toolkit, the phases are intended as a framework as well as a platform for practitioners to build and tailor contextual evaluations on the basis of their practice, service, worksite, sector and the evaluation brief.

Well-designed evaluations can impact on service development and funding decisions, inform policy making and research initiatives, and provide platforms for subsequent evaluation cycles (Figure 2).

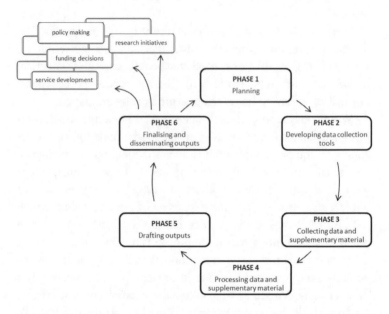

FIGURE 2 EVALUATION PHASES

## A note on terminology

The practices encompassed within the arts therapies and arts & health are diverse, distinct and overlapping. In order to avoid discipline- or practice-specific jargon, and for the sake of consistency, the following terms are used throughout this guide:

**Arts-based**
Any kind of arts-related practice.

**Evaluator**
Used interchangeably with practitioner throughout the guide, on the understanding that the evaluator may not always be the practitioner, and vice versa.

**Practitioner**
Any arts therapy and arts & health professional or student, such as art, drama, music or dance movement therapists, integral arts psychotherapists, creative arts psychotherapists, community musicians and artists, arts in health practitioners.

**Project**
In order to distinguish between evaluation and arts-based work, we restrict the term 'projects' to evaluation, and use 'services' to signify arts-based work.

**Service**
Any practices, projects or services irrespective of their media (e.g. music, visual arts, dance, writing), formats (e.g. work with individuals, small or large group) or longevity (e.g. long-term or short-term services, including one-off projects).

**Service user**
People (irrespective of age, culture or condition) who access the service, such as arts therapy clients, hospital patients, care home residents, project participants and so on.

Finally, throughout this guide, services are described as being provided within the context of organisations (i.e. a workplace or site). However, the evaluation principles presented apply equally to arts-based practitioners working as consultants, across a number of organisations or as independent professionals.

# Evaluation Basics

Not evaluating is not an option. Practitioners have no option but to evaluate proactively, and even if not leading on or driving evaluations themselves, it is necessary to be well informed enough to be closely involved and vigilant when participating in externally driven evaluations about their projects and practices. In the UK, for instance, arts therapists are registered with the Health and Care Professions Council (HCPC), which specifies that evaluating practice and participating in audit procedures, maintaining records, keeping and managing accurate, comprehensive and comprehensible records is an essential part of the HCPC Standards of Proficiency (HCPC, 2013). Not evaluating is not an option.

This chapter provides some conceptual anchors to underpin the evaluation journey, distinguishing between monitoring, evaluation, audit and research, before focusing on the various purposes and functions of evaluation. Having considered some of the impulses that inform the evaluation brief (i.e. questions such as 'Who is the evaluation for? What does its focus need to be? Who will read it? And what is its broader contextual purpose?'), the chapter concludes with some reflections on the challenges of representing arts-based services, and on the shifting and drifting nature of reality, truth, evidence and fact, arguing that context is all, and the service, the method and the design need to be a coherent and cohesive entity.

## Why evaluate? Who and what is evaluation for?

These are slightly different questions and already hint at the manifold nature of the evaluation exercise. This guide contends that the first question – 'Why evaluate?' – cannot be answered without the second – 'Who and what is evaluation for?'

The evaluation brief may come from sponsors, clients, managers, staff or other – not always evident – stakeholders. Each of these groups will have individual interests, which will impact on the evaluation's design and method. Since evaluations may well impact on decision making, keeping in mind the type of decisions that need to be made from the very beginning of the evaluation project is critical, since evaluation inevitably has a political agenda, however tacit. One-size-fits-all evaluation procedures, while saving time and resources, may not always be the best option once the evaluation brief has been elicited.

There are various possible scenarios that constitute the evaluation brief, some of which are presented in Figure 3 below as if they are definitive and separate rationales for evaluation. While this separation is useful when considering the main focus of an evaluation, in everyday life the scenarios are inevitably interlinked.

FIGURE 3 EVALUATION BRIEF SCENARIOS

## Scenario 1: Quality of service provision

The evaluation seeks to ensure that a service is delivering a quality practice, working to the best possible efficiency, using the organisational resources optimally, and contributing effectively to the site of work and to the service users.

## Scenario 2: Finances and publicity

The evaluation aims to make a case for continued financial support and possibly for an expansion of the service. The evaluation findings may also be used for public petitioning or campaigning, publicity and advocacy. Evaluations can also be designed to test the effect of funding policies and politics on arts-based practices.

## Scenario 3: Project management

The evaluation seeks to ensure that a service is proceeding according to its aims and objectives; helping to identify unexpected developments or gaps; and helping to reframe the service where there is a change in funding. It can also be an early-warning system if something is not going according to plan, and helps to justify implementation of remedial actions.

## Scenario 4: Service delivery standards

Robust and systematic data collected from an evaluation may well set standards for the current and future service delivery; some organisations call this benchmarking. While this may not be the original impetus, it may form part of the unintended consequences of an evaluation project, and is worth keeping in mind when considering the function of the evaluation.

## Scenario 5: Replication of service

Evaluations can be commissioned because managers are considering introducing a similar service in another locality, sector or department within the organisation. Here, the evaluation provides a guide for planning and implementing a new and similar service.

### Scenario 6: Value for money

While value for money generally forms an implicit part of the evaluation brief, evaluations are frequently requested to test that allocated funds are being spent efficiently. While evaluation is not necessarily (or specifically) an accounting exercise, by assessing whether or not the service is fulfilling the aims on the basis of which the funding was allocated, it is possible to assess the extent to which the service is value for money. This reassures stakeholders and contributes to preventing fraud.

### Scenario 7: User satisfaction and equal opportunities

Evaluations offer service users the opportunity to record their experiences of the project/service, helping to assess the project, learn from it and inform developments and replications. Evaluations are as much for the benefit of service users as for persons in policy and decision-making positions. Evaluation enables service users' voices to be heard and can help ensure that managers and funders communicate directly with the service users. It can be a positive, affirming experience for participants in the project, who are perhaps often overlooked when it comes to valuing their voice.

The scenarios above already suggest the elements of advocacy and activism that are inherent in evaluation. Evaluation is never value-free. It seeks to influence practice, helping to identify potential pathways for the future and contributing to the next planning phases of a service.

Since arts-based services are characterised and experienced as dynamically and temporally shifting and since generating data for evaluations involves people whose experiences will change over time, assigning fixed evaluative criteria is a complicated business. This does not mean that it is to be avoided, but rather that a rigorous model needs to be in place to make sense of evaluative information. One possibility is to consider evaluation as an ongoing dynamic cycle, during which value-led practices and evaluative information are rigorously documented and studied and revisited cyclically. The building of such cycles is based on the understanding that services and values are contingent on the experiences and values of stakeholders, participants and practitioners – where such experiences are systematically documented and assessed. Participant Action Research methodology, with the Plan–Act–Observe–Reflect spiral at its heart (Figure 4), offers a frame for conceptualising the assimilation of experiences of participants and stakeholders, and for signalling the ongoing dynamic nature of values embedded in the arts (Stige, 2005; Westhues *et al.*, 2008).

FIGURE 4 THE PLAN–ACT–OBSERVE–REFLECT SPIRAL

## Representing arts-based practices: audiences (and discourses)

Arts therapists and arts & health practitioners value a fleeting new expression on a service user's face, a moment of electric connection with an isolated person, a breath that signals intention to vocalise, or the slight movement of a finger of a physically disabled patient that signals possible cognitive awareness. However, funders, business managers or hospital directors may value the number of service users being seen each day by the practitioner, the rate of development of those service users or the reduction of symptoms in order to assess whether the service represents value for money. These different value systems carry equal importance. The attention to detail and knowledge and care a practitioner has for service users is very important, yet it is equally important to be able to see whether and how people are benefitting from the service and how many people are impacted. Although working at different levels, both managers and practitioners have the quality of the service in mind. Different yet equally relevant agendas and values need to be represented within evaluation outputs through a range of types of information. In this way, a picture of the service can be shown and appreciated as fully as possible.

While holding readers in mind is a useful barometer for helping to collect and process data, evaluations tend to have distinct audiences who will be seeking particular kinds of evidence. While it is impossible to consider everybody's needs, expectations and interests, it is strategic to identify primary audiences early on. Considering the audience(s), as well as their contexts, values and expertise, directly affects the kind of data practitioners need, how much data they collect and from whom, and how they represent the evaluation through different outputs, language style and vocabulary.

The funders or commissioners of a service are likely to have the most vested interests in the outcomes, possibly reading it through their (at times, hidden) agendas. Managers and budget holders look for evidence that speaks to their priorities, while other audiences may be reading the report for collegial, advocacy, professional or disciplinary interests: they may be more interested in what they can learn about the service than its efficient use of funds.

Readers may well be assessing the evaluation outputs on the basis of specific vocabulary. For example, the term 'impact' has become very popular over the past decade in relation to the increased focus on evidence-based practice. 'Impact' has become a key term in the policy-making and funding world, and it is often associated with evaluation of services in the context of 'assessing impact'. Although an increased number of practitioners are asked to demonstrate their services' impact, many of them have no clear understanding of what 'impact' actually means.

> Impacts are actual or intended changes in human development as measured by people's well-being. Impacts generally capture changes in people's lives. (United Nations Development Programme, 2009, p.56)

Impact is particularly appropriate for the evaluative context since it carries meaning of change yet assumes no value of change and also has no negative or positive implication. As a neutral term, it is useful to use when reporting on evaluation outcomes.

However, part of the complications around reporting arts-based practices is the vexing and – at times – unresolvable issue around representation.

Arts therapists and arts & health practitioners are familiar with the difficulties of representing their work through the written page. The tensions around representation of any of the arts through – in this instance – words and numbers touch on issues of translations and hybridity. What happens to people's experiences of music, to an image, to movement or dance when these are transformed into 'value for money', 'project management' and 'finances and publicity'? Equally, how do budget variances, management-speak and local government policies translate into musical performances, paintings or poetry?

While even the best and closest documentations remain representative of the service, evaluations straddle multiple representations, needing to convey the character and value of the service and translate these into the logic of written language and numbers. While, for practitioners and service users, evaluation outputs seem to replace, reduce, airbrush, sanitise or skew the events and experiences, they need to be seen in context, as one of the range of complementary – and overlapping – representations. Moreover, including supplementary material (such as images and vignettes) into evaluation outputs often complements the more distancing kinds of representations and may be the very sections that appeal to service users, their families and advocacy groups.

As is becoming apparent, the evaluation journey consists of a number of activities with individual timeframes. Evaluation also may exist alongside other evidence-gathering activities, some of which may be overlapping or distinct from each other. Monitoring, evaluation, audit and research are four main evidence-gathering activities. While presenting these four values-based activities as separate and distinct is intended to help stabilise both the vocabularies and tasks, and to retain this guide's focus on evaluation, their close relationship and overlaps need to be kept in mind.

## Monitoring, evaluation, audit and research

In their handbook for development practitioners, Kusek and Rist (2004) consider the roles of evaluation for socioeconomic development and public management, presenting the distinction between evaluations whose focus is internal to a project (i.e. implementation-focused, which this guide does not address) and those whose focus straddles the project results and their contexts (i.e. the project's impact on the 'outside world').

> Results-based monitoring and evaluation (M&E) is a powerful public management tool that can be used to help policymakers and decision-makers track progress and demonstrate the impact of a given project, program, or policy. Results-based M&E differs from traditional implementation-focused M&E in that it moves beyond an emphasis on inputs and outputs to a greater focus on outcomes and impacts. (Kusek and Rist, 2004, p.1)

For arts-based practitioners, results-based evaluation answers the all-too-familiar 'so what' questions, and often challenges assumptions about what is of value, to whom, at what time and for what purpose:

> Credible answers to the 'so what' question address the accountability concerns of stakeholders, give public sector managers information on progress toward achieving stated targets and goals, and provide substantial evidence as the basis for any necessary mid-course corrections in policies, programs, or projects. (Kusek and Rist, 2004, p.12)

Crucially, the timing of evaluations is a moveable feat: acting on their informed intuitions, practitioners may decide not to wait for the completion of projects, or for deadlines that are externally imposed. Proactive timings can help to signal that services might be going off-track (and provide opportunities to alter course well before the end of a project delivery); that aspects of services might need more or less emphasis in order to ensure optimal use of resources; that project funders need to be alerted to changes in anticipated impact; and so on.

Like any service delivery, arts-based practices are situated in and are part of social, cultural and organisational contexts, each of which has unique value systems and distinct understandings of 'impact', 'evidence' and 'effectiveness'. Organisations and funders may well have preferred and pre-existing frameworks for conveying these understandings, of which evaluation is one. Table 1 presents the various pathways to evidence gathering (Farrant, Pavlicevic and Tsiris, 2014).

Each of these different pathways to evidence gathering has distinct functions and purposes; no one pathway is more powerful or efficient than the other – this depends on context and purpose! Practitioners need to consider which pathway is appropriate for their service, within the context of the organisation, the resources available, the nature of the practice, the time available and how best to complement any other impact/evidence goings-on in the organisation. These kinds of considerations help to ensure optimal efficiency: the right level of activity at the right time, and the right kind of information. In other words, like arts-based services, any evaluative enterprise needs to be fit-for-purpose.

**TABLE 1 Characteristics of monitoring, evaluation, audit and research**

| | Monitoring | Evaluation | Audit | Research |
|---|---|---|---|---|
| Aims | To document systems, people or organisations over time | To assess a service | To assess whether a service is following predetermined standards of best practice | To contribute to disciplinary and cross-disciplinary practices, theory and knowledge |
| Objectives | Notes emerging trends over time without determination of merit or worth | Assesses the service/project in relation to its aims | Assesses the service against pre-set organisational benchmarks | Addresses defined questions, aims and objectives |
| Impact | Implications for the service development and its context (site/sector/funder/practice) | | | Implications for practice, professional and disciplinary scholarship |
| Participants | Persons directly or indirectly affected by the service (e.g. service users, families, staff, funders) | | | Selected purposively or randomly, depending on project aims, methodology and design |
| Intervention | Captures information on ongoing basis through a range of tools | Assesses existing information and generates additional data through standardised or bespoke tools | | Uses a variety of research techniques and methods in a range of settings |
| Research ethics | Research ethics review not necessarily required, but ethical implications need to be discussed with an ethics representative within the organisation | | | REC approval is required |

Although evaluation is closely linked to monitoring (as 'monitoring and evaluation', or 'M&E'), the two are distinct activities. Monitoring generally happens as a matter of course and involves entering service information on a regular basis in attendance registers, session notes and checklists, or recording/filming sessions and activities. By assembling targeted information over time, monitoring enables trends to be identified within a timeframe, which information may well help to trigger and plan an evaluation. For example, monitoring may reveal a certain trend in one aspect of the service (attendance on Monday afternoons is declining, while Friday evening provisions are more popular). Having noted the trend, an evaluation exercise may then aim to elicit explanations for this trend, and assess whether or not that aspect of the service needs to be adapted, expanded or stopped.

Since monitoring and evaluation are not limited to arts-based services, and although nomenclature is not always stable, it may be useful to consider various definitions from a range of sectors and disciplines, in order to assemble and elucidate their meanings.

Here are four definitions of each, from a range of sectors, some more distant from the arts than others.

> Monitoring is a continuous function that uses the systematic collection of data on specified indicators to provide management and the main stakeholders of an ongoing development intervention with indications of the extent of progress and achievement of objectives and progress in the use of allocated funds. (OECD, 2002, p.27, cited in Kusek and Rist, 2004, p.12)

> Monitoring is defined as the routine collection and use of data to assess progress in achieving programme objectives. These data are generally derived from programme records. (Bristol-Myers Squibb Foundation, undated, p.57)

> Monitoring can be defined as a continuing function that aims primarily to provide the management and main stakeholders of an on-going intervention with early indications of progress,

or lack thereof, in the achievement of results. An on-going intervention might be a project, program or other kind of support to an outcome. Monitoring helps organizations track achievements by a regular collection of information to assist timely decision making, ensure accountability, and provide the basis for evaluation and learning. (Sera and Beaudry, 2007, p.1)

Monitoring is a continuing function that uses the systematic collection of data on specified indicators to inform management and the main stakeholders of [...] the extent of progress and achievement of results in the use of allocated funds [...] (United Nations World Food Programme, undated, p.9)

The emphasis from these four definitions is the longitudinal, routine aspect of monitoring with its continuous tracking function. In other words, monitoring is not a haphazard spontaneous or ad hoc collection of information, but is planned systematically in advance. The information to be collected is targeted for particular purposes. However, the information is not put through a systematic assessment exercise – which is one of the functions of evaluation.

Evaluation is the systematic and objective assessment of an ongoing or completed project, program, or policy, including its design, implementation, and results. The aim is to determine the relevance and fulfillment of objectives, development efficiency, effectiveness, impact, and sustainability. An evaluation should provide information that is credible and useful, enabling the incorporation of lessons learned into the decision making process of both recipients and donors. (OECD, 2002, p.21, cited in Kusek and Rist, 2004, p.12)

Evaluation involves collecting special data on a periodic or 'as needed' basis to address issues that cannot be examined using routinely collected data, like a project's cost-effectiveness or overall impact. (Bristol-Myers Squibb Foundation, undated, p.57)

Evaluation is the systematic and objective assessment of an on-going or completed project, program, or policy, and its design, implementation and results. The aim is to determine the relevance and fulfillment of objectives, development efficiency, effectiveness, impact, and sustainability. An evaluation should provide information that is credible and useful, enabling the incorporation of lessons learned into the decision making process of both recipients and donors. (Sera and Beaudry, 2007, p.1)

Evaluation is the systematic and objective assessment of an on-going or completed operation, programme or policy, its design, implementation and results. The aim is to determine the relevance and fulfillment of objectives, as well as efficiency, effectiveness, impact and sustainability. (United Nations World Food Programme, undated, p.9)

In contrast to monitoring, evaluation assesses information. It is more than a collection of facts over time and more than a representation of facts in particular formats. Evaluation is a systematic intentional procedure that processes collected data and 'tests' it according to value criteria.

## Integrating evaluation into practice and contexts

Although evaluation covers a range of activities, the focus of evaluation in this guide is on identifying and assessing the value(s) of a service embedded within its contexts. Evaluation, here, avoids considering the service as an isolated, decontextualised activity or world. On the contrary, the aims, procedures and function of evaluation are understood as dependent on audience; usually it is the stakeholders associated with the service who may have requested the evaluation in the first instance. These can be funders, donors, managers, advocacy groups, professional organisations.

Evaluation helps to assess the extent to which the service is fulfilling its original aims, in a particular context, at a particular time – and these aims will often have been negotiated together with the stakeholders at the start of the service. By helping to identify aspects of the service that work well (and need to be developed), that are unsuccessful (and need to be changed or stopped) and that need attention (and need to be adapted or restarted), evaluations help to ensure that the service is fit-for-purpose, offers value for money and meets the standards of best possible quality of practice and service delivery.

While it is common for practitioners to be asked for evaluations – or evidence – by service managers, or as part of the service delivery, it is less common for practitioners to instigate evaluations on their own initiative. This is understandable, given that evaluation requires specific skills and uses precious time and energy.

In the book *Beginning Research in the Arts Therapies*, Ansdell and Pavlicevic write about the experience of a novice researcher, which is also true for a novice evaluator:

> Be reassured straight away that a certain amount of panic is only to be expected if you've trained primarily as a practitioner in an arts therapy and suddenly find, for whatever reason, you need to do [evaluation] […] only in recent years have arts therapists become involved in [evaluating] their own work (rather than have it [evaluated] by professional evaluators). (adapted from Ansdell and Pavlicevic, 2001, pp.9–10)

By collecting information about the service regularly and in a targeted manner (such as monitoring and feedback procedures), practitioners are well on the way to building information platforms (or banks) as part of their practice from the very beginning. Even before beginning the evaluative process, this ongoing assembling of information ensures that practitioners are not caught unawares.

This ongoing foraging and assembling of information is dependent on practitioners developing a distinctive perspective as part of their work. While practitioners are already skilled at being wholly engaged in the arts-based activities while concurrently alert to the quality and level of participants' engagements (and addressing these as needed), the additional evaluative stance can be understood as slightly more distant and more global. The evaluative stance oversees the entire work as it happens and while also being closely and minutely engaged in the arts-based practice and its processes. Through sustaining these multiple stances, the practitioner records and sifts the unfolding events, then monitors these and assigns them value, documenting on an ongoing basis. Monitoring is more than attendance and absence registers, and session plans and descriptions. It is a distinctive stance that kindles alertness to evaluative criteria and processes, based on the very arts-based activities as these unfold over time. In this way, it is the arts-based work that itself contributes to the planning of systematic and rigorous evaluations.

Monitoring alone rarely suffices. However, since monitoring is a crucial platform for evaluation, a sustained integrated monitoring stance guarantees that practitioners will feel more 'in control' and better placed to ensure 'ownership' when beginning the evaluation process, irrespective of who asks for the evaluations and when.

## Evaluation with attitude

Since embarking on an evaluation journey demands stamina and dedication, and may at times feel like a distraction from the primary activity of delivering services and projects, here are some key 'attitudes' guaranteed to enhance and enrich the evaluation journey.

## Constructive and courageous

Being constructive is not the same as ignoring or sidestepping difficult issues. When some organisations or projects (for reasons that are not always clear) become trapped in spirals of negativity, these impact on the evaluation: for instance, staff or service users will 'forget' appointments to participate in the evaluation, be consistently late, make pointed jokes or gossip about colleagues. Without vigilance, such enactments become draining, and the practitioner risks running out of energy and feeling unsupported. Being constructive means facing difficulties head on, being vigilant about micro-politics and courageous enough to address them, and conveying to all involved in the evaluation that their participation and input is valued and respected, no matter how difficult they might find their contribution. Being constructive in other words is to do with respect, alertness and with making the evaluation agenda as explicit as possible.

## Expecting the unexpected

Even where the evaluation is well planned, nothing quite works out the way it was intended to. An attitude of flexibility (which often characterises arts-based practices), and an openness to being surprised, and to learning, undoubtedly enriches the evaluation experience for everybody.

## Genuine interest and curiosity

These qualities help to retain a sense of freshness and energy, even during phases that might feel mechanical and rather uncreative.

## Creative spirit of inquiry

This is linked to being courageous. Where evaluations are often considered a rather dull version of research, by retaining their creative spiritedness, arts-based practitioners are particularly well resourced for ensuring an imaginative and thorough grasp of evaluation information.

### Negative capability[4]

This can be a coping resource in managing uncertainty, of which there will almost certainly be plenty – for example, in relation to uncooperative staff members, delays in receiving written informed consent, unclear organisational dynamics, and more. Negative capability allows practitioners to couple their decisive actions, with 'reflective inaction' when needed (Simpson, French and Harvey, 2002).

### Sustaining a 'healthy' attitude

Although what constitutes health is hardly the focus of this guide, three aspects borrowed from Antonovsky's 'salutogenic' model of health (1996) are helpful to bear in mind for one's healthy engagement with evaluation:

- *Comprehensibility:* Understanding what evaluation is and how it works, knowing how to employ different evaluation methods, procedures, and being open to revising these constantly.

- *Manageability:* Ensuring that as evaluators, practitioners have the right skills and relevant resources for their evaluation project. Closely linked to knowledge and understanding, the practical ability to implement the evaluation needs both human and material resources. Practitioners need to remain reflexive about the possibilities as well as the limitations afforded by available resources.

- *Meaningfulness:* Finding personal meaning and motivation is vital for engaging positively with evaluation while, paradoxically, retaining the necessary evaluator's distance. Since being motivated and inspired is contagious, this increases the chances of wholehearted involvement in the evaluation by others (i.e. as participants or collaborators).

---

4   Originally John Keats's term to describe the artist's receptiveness to the world, used later by Wilfred Bion to illustrate an attitude of openness and the ability to tolerate not knowing, rather than imposing ready-made or omnipotent certainties upon ambiguous situations or challenges (French, 2001).

The synergies that make for successful evaluations will be much enhanced by such attitudes, which can be considered part of the stabilising foundational platform needed to sustain the at times long-winded evaluation journey (and to prevent entropy).

## Between experience, reality, evidence and...truth

> There is no doubt fiction makes a better job of the truth.
>
> *Doris Lessing,* Under My Skin

> The truth is always something that is told, not something that is known. If there were no speaking or writing, there would be no truth about anything. There would only be what is.
>
> *Susan Sontag,* The Benefactor

There are many truths...and truths have many tellings. Truths are contingent on context, time, politics and who creates them.

All evaluation is political – whether seeking to confirm good practice, show the need for change, sustain the status quo at all costs and so on. To complicate matters further, many organisational and political sensitivities are hidden from view.

The questions below may feel as though they belong only to the early phases of an evaluation. By retaining and reviewing these constantly, throughout the evaluation phases, they act as a radar, continuously scanning the project, the service, the organisation, and help to remain alert to complications surrounding any and all aspects of the evaluation project.

- What kind of evidence is being sought?
- What values drive the evidence?
- What are the pressures (implicit or explicit)?
- Who may be dis/empowered as a result of this project?
- What will be learnt from this evaluation?

- What assurances are there that the project outputs will be circulated?

- What assurances are there that the recommendations deriving from the evaluation outcomes will be acted upon?

- What assurances are there that the evaluation will make a difference?

- Who controls what happens to the recommendations?

As discussed later, the question of who takes part in the evaluation (and who does not) can be one of the subtle political strategies surrounding an evaluation. Here are some more scanning questions:

- Who is participating in the evaluation – and who is not – and why?

- How can all stakeholders' interests be represented and balanced?

- Are all views represented – positive, negative, critical, flattering, disinterested, etc.?

- How will personal and organisational agendas be balanced?

- Whose discourse(s) will be prominent? (And whose discourses will remain invisible?)

- What other questions need to be asked?

Although some of these questions pertain to the evaluation, to only consider them at the writing-up stage is too late. They need to be part of the evaluation from the very beginning when the evaluation brief is being negotiated. Once the evaluation is under way, if the evaluation is to be worth the effort and resources invested in it, new questions may present themselves and need to be faced, however uncomfortable they may be.

Evaluations walk a delicate line in response to briefing values and agendas, while seeking not to compromise the character and experiences of arts-based practices. What data is assembled, and how and when, will be framed – and to some extent predetermined – by the truth(s) shaped by the evaluation brief. Collecting data can combine assembling quotations from notes and reflective journals, writing up vignettes, carrying out interviews, as well as compiling regular log-sheets and attendance records. A range of evaluation data, some numeric, narrative or pictorial, collected from a range of people (such as the practitioner, service users, service users' parents or family members, staff or carers, and managers), helps to ensure that whatever truths are told through evaluation, they are constructed on the basis of as near to a 360-degree scan of multiple evidence as possible.

Having set out the 'evaluation basics', the following chapters focus on the practicalities and the steps for each evaluation phase. Although the information provided in each phase is detailed, by no means is it the *alpha* and *omega* of evaluation journeys. On the contrary, practitioners are invited to develop their evaluative stance throughout this guide, and engage with the information critically and contextually. It is through prioritising the specifics of a service, organisation and evaluation brief over – and in tandem with – the phased life cycle of an evaluative framework that evaluation will retain the freshness, integrity and creativity that inspires arts-based practices.

# Phase 1

## Planning

Plans are nothing; planning is everything.

*Dwight D. Eisenhower*

Evaluation demands efficient planning, and planning is time-consuming. Some negative perceptions about evaluation may stem from a feeling that it involves a lot of effort, that this is not part of a practitioner's skill set, and that much information is gathered needlessly. However, time spent planning helps to avoid wasting energy and resources.

It is strategic to ensure close alignment between the context, the service, the evaluation timelines, the data collection tools, and explicit or implicit values and agendas. All these dimensions need to be considered from the very beginning of designing an evaluation project (which at times may or may not coincide with the establishment of a service).

## 1.1 Evaluation foundations

Planning helps to establish the evaluation foundations, and Phase 1 presents eight main dimensions that need to be covered as part of planning:

- evaluation aims and objectives
- participants

- evaluator(s)
- timelines
- evaluation budget
- regulations and formalities
- consent
- dissemination.

## Evaluation aims and objectives

The evaluation aims and objectives need to be drafted from the start in relation to the service aims and objectives. The former can be informed by early meetings with managers and/or funders who will signal their interests and agendas for the evaluation. By teasing out the differences and overlaps between service aims, objectives and evaluation aims, practitioners clarify not only the scope of evaluation, but also its limitations: what the evaluation *does not* aim to do. Table 2 provides various examples of how organisational/service aims can relate to certain service objectives and evaluation aims. As these emerge, organisational/service aims relate to 'what' questions, service objectives to 'how' questions, and evaluation aims to 'what to evaluate' questions.

Once an evaluation procedure has begun, a wealth of possibilities and additional evaluation aims may well present themselves. While alert to these possibilities, practitioners can ensure that the evaluation retains its focus and does not go 'off piste' – for example, by developing new aims or collecting data that does not address the original evaluation aims. It may well be that additional possibilities will enrich the evaluation outputs and form part of recommendations for future project objectives.

**TABLE 2 Examples of link between organisational/ service aims, service objectives and evaluation aims**

| Organisational/ service aims | Service objectives | Evaluation aims |
|---|---|---|
| To pilot music therapy at Darndell House | To deliver 50 hours of music therapy to service users at Darndell House, over a period of three months | To check that the service is delivered within the stated timeframe |
| To improve the organisational health and wellbeing at Darndell House | To institute Sunday afternoon tea dances for staff, residents and visitors/families | To assess the impact of Sunday afternoon tea dances at Darndell House |
| To increase service users' participation in local community activities | To institute weekly community choir rehearsals To institute choir performances in local events | To evaluate the impact of the choir project upon service users' participation in community activities |
| To enrich communication and relationships between staff and service users | To develop joint staff–service user weekly painting groups | To assess the impact of the weekly painting groups |
| To establish the arts therapies as part of the multidisciplinary team | To develop systems that ensure information flow between all multidisciplinary team members | To assess information flow between all members of the multidisciplinary team |

## *Participants: whom to involve?*

Knowing whom and how many to involve as evaluation participants can be difficult: service users, staff, service users' family members, other arts practitioners, managers, or all of the above? Rather than assuming that everyone needs to be involved from the start, a clear strategy focuses on who (and how many) might provide the fullest range of information and for what purpose. While there is no formula, various combinations of these considerations need to be taken into account.

- *The commissioner's requirements.* A good understanding of what the commissioner of the evaluation requires, and whose 'voice' they value. For example, many commissioners value most highly the personal opinion of the service users themselves, while others are more focused on that of senior staff members.

- *The kind of organisation.* In privately-funded care, where the families of service users pay for services directly, the opinions of family members and residents may be the most sought after, while in medical institutions it may be that the voices of the medical staff are most valued. Organisations whose staff work different shifts can be an evaluation minefield, because of the inaccessibility of staff.

- *The type of service being evaluated.* A short-term project, for example, may need to target those directly involved, rather than attempt to elicit information from everyone in a (large) organisation.

- *The evaluation aims.* This is the best barometer! There is no point targeting a broad range of persons if the aim can be addressed by a targeted group, who can be selected specifically because of their particular activities, roles, status and availability.

- *The timeframe.* A one-off project, such as a Christmas concert, limits opportunities for evaluation, especially where instant feedback is sought. Paper feedback forms on seats are not everyone's priority, particularly when refreshments follow the concert.

- *The politics of organisational status and roles.* While in many institutions the voice of those with particular professional roles carry substantial weight, part of the politics of evaluation may well be to ensure a 360-degree representation of stakeholders. This may mean involving people drawn from a range of organisational roles (e.g. medical consultant, finance manager, care staff and volunteers) in addition to the service users – or, on the contrary (and always depending on the brief and the aims!), the evaluation aim may best be addressed through targeting evaluation participants from a specific service role (e.g. choir members). In addition to considering organisational roles, it may be helpful to consider how close or distant potential evaluation participants are from the service (see Figure 5).

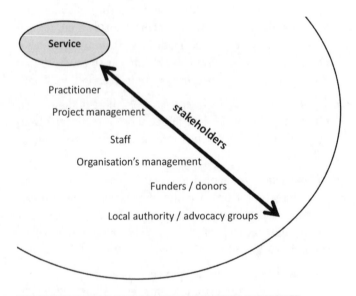

FIGURE 5 EVALUATION PARTICIPANTS' PROXIMITY TO THE SERVICE

- *Service users' resilience and vulnerabilities.* Many arts therapists and arts & health practitioners work with vulnerable people, who are often an excellent source from which to gather first-hand information about the service. However, there are practical and ethical implications of involving vulnerable people in evaluations, including their mental capacity, capabilities and the risk of burdening them with the responsibility. These aspects need to be considered from the start – to help inform the choices of data collection methods and the length and questions asked in data collection tools. A terminally ill patient or a bereaved family member may not be in a state of mind to complete questionnaires, just as a person with severe learning disabilities may find it very difficult or impossible to complete a written form. In addition, there are established ethical guidelines for involving vulnerable people as evaluation participants, which need to be considered as early on as possible (Farrant, Pavlicevic and Tsiris, 2014; Tsiris and Hartley, 2013). While adding complications to the time and processes of collecting evaluation material, the benefits of involving service participants will be self-evident.

## Evaluator(s)[5]

Most smaller organisations or services opt to conduct evaluations internally due to budget constraints. However, it may be worth considering consulting an external evaluator familiar with arts-based practices to advise, especially at the planning stages, and perhaps to help with some of the later phases (such as collecting

---

5   Since this guide is addressed to arts therapists and arts & health practitioners, the 'evaluator' is assumed to be the practitioner in all the following sections and examples. However, evaluation is inevitably a collaborative venture, and where the practitioner is the main or 'lead' evaluator, a supportive network with a sense of common ownership of the evaluation is invaluable.

and processing data). This may be somebody external to the organisation who is well versed in arts-based practices, or somebody internal to the organisation but less familiar with the practice or service. While this possibility depends on funding, skills base and timeframe, being informed of the benefits and limitations of internal and external evaluators helps to make informed decisions.

Internal evaluators are part of the organisational structure. They have pre-existing relationships with staff and service users involved, and are familiar with the service's context and the organisational sensitivities and politics. However, this familiarity can affect the evaluator's reflective capacity and limit their awareness of shared assumptions in the organisation – something which at times may hinder the effectiveness of the evaluation. In such cases, an outsider's perspective is helpful. External evaluators are often viewed by funders as providing a more distant and fresh look at the service. In addition, external evaluators may provide evaluation expertise and experience from other evaluation projects in diverse settings. On the other hand, external evaluators may require time to develop trust among staff and evaluation participants may have poor understanding of the arts-based practice itself and impose 'incompatible' methodological frameworks (Feuerstein, 1986; Wadsworth, 2011). Also, cost implications need to be considered in the choice between internal and external evaluators. In this guide, the emphasis is given on arts-based practitioners acting as internal evaluators.

### Timelines

The six chronological phases of evaluation in this guide help to develop a timeline for the evaluation. The most important piece of information from the start is the final submission deadline for the delivery of the evaluation outputs (e.g. the evaluation report submission date). This may be based on crucial funding application deadlines, so it is vital that the submission deadline is clearly established from the start. A timeline for the evaluation project is then created through working backwards from this deadline and consequently calculating how much time is available for each phase of the evaluation. This will, in turn, determine the design of the evaluation – that is, the size and scale of the evaluation, how much and how the data is collected. Setting deadlines for every phase of the evaluation keeps the delivery of the final outputs on schedule. Since evaluations take time and effort, it is important to be realistic and not underestimate the amount of time each of these phases takes. In addition, personal workload (including how many days on site) and the pace of life at the organisation need to be considered when setting timelines.

Taking each of these into consideration from the start is very much part of the planning process. Table 3 gives examples of factors that influence the length of each evaluation phase. Generally, practitioners' time availability and the size and complexity of the evaluation underpin timelines.

## TABLE 3 Timeframe considerations
## for each evaluation phase

| Phases | What dictates the time needed to complete each evaluation phase? |
|---|---|
| Phase 1: Planning | Depends on the availability of essential information:<br><br>• How efficient is the information on the evaluation brief? And how efficient is the communication with evaluation commissioners for additional information?<br>• How efficient is the information flow within the organisation?<br>• How accessible are the key staff members within the organisation?<br>• How long will it take to get any necessary approval for conducting the evaluation and/or for use of material such as photos or audio extracts? |
| Phase 2: Developing data collection tools | Depends on the practitioner's pace of work and how many people must approve the tools:<br><br>• How long will it take to check the data collection tools with the relevant people (e.g. a line manager) and make any changes? |
| Phase 3: Collecting data and supplementary material | Depends on methods, amount of data and material needed, and time onsite:<br><br>• Are all the interviewees onsite on the same day?<br>• How long will it take people to complete and return questionnaires?<br>• How frequently and regularly is the practitioner onsite? (Only half a day per week may mean that several weeks are needed compared to a week's intensive evaluation.)<br>• When are the school 'term dates'?<br>• Are any vital evaluation participants on annual leave? |

| | |
|---|---|
| **Phase 4: Processing data and supplementary material** | Depends on the amount and format of data and material collected and on the processing resources:<br><br>• How much data and material has been collected?<br>• Who will transcribe interview recordings?<br>• How will the data and material collected be collated, organised and presented? |
| **Phase 5: Drafting outputs** | Depends on the required evaluation outputs, their type, detail and size:<br><br>• Have sections of the evaluation report already been written while waiting for questionnaires to be returned?<br>• How long will it take to check the full report, leaflets or other outputs with line managers? |
| **Phase 6: Finalising and disseminating outputs** | Depends on the submission requirements of the evaluation 'audience':<br><br>• Does the audience require electronic or paper copies of the evaluation report?<br>• Do confidentiality agreements prohibit emailing evaluation outputs?<br>• Do the leaflets reporting on the evaluation outcomes need to be sent to an external printer, and, if so, how long does the printing take? |

## *Evaluation budget*

All evaluations need funding, whether delineated for the (external) evaluator's time or whether the practitioner is funded for evaluation time as part of the service. Additional funding that may emerge later in the evaluation process includes human resources (e.g. practitioners' case workload and evaluation skills, working hours, attendance of relevant training) and material resources (e.g. number of photocopies, purchase of data analysis software). All possible funding needs to form part of the evaluation budget at the planning stage.

## Regulations and formalities

Many organisations have internal formalities or regulations that are not necessarily evident to part-time practitioners or when providing services for a fixed term. It is during the planning stages that these need to be elicited; for example, some organisations do not allow questionnaires to be distributed to service users unless they have been approved by, for example, an internal committee; other organisations do not allow any questionnaires or interviews to take place with staff during working hours; or there may be strict formalities about what contact with service users is and is not allowed. Some larger organisations may want to review the ethical aspects of the evaluation before it begins, requiring a proposal. For example, any evaluations that take place within NHS hospitals need to adhere to the Caldicott principles which delineate the ethical principles by which all research or evaluative activity must abide. It is worth flagging up, however, that in some cases organisations may require the evaluation proposal to include the relevant data collection tools, in which case the proposal could be completed after Phase 2.

Any such formalities inevitably affect the evaluation timeframe and design, and need to be known during the planning stages.

## Consent

Whether or not it is part of the regulations and (legal) formalities that exist in an organisation, seeking consent from evaluation participants is always best practice and safeguards both evaluators and participants. In addition, if artwork (e.g. paintings, poems, audio recordings) which is beyond the evaluative context (e.g. has been provided/generated during art-therapy sessions) is needed as supplementary material for the evaluation, consent will inevitably be needed from those involved or depicted in the photos. The gaining of consent can be a lengthy process, and asking for consent needs to begin as early as possible in the evaluation process (for more information on ethics, see 'A Note on Ethics', page 161).

Although the reason for doing an evaluation project may be to secure funding for the continuation of the service or in order to replicate the same service in another geographical region, thinking of other possibilities is important, especially since obtaining permissions for broader use of information retrospectively is not good practice and can be a complex (or even an impossible) process.

If it is likely that the evaluation project will attract the attention of communication and fundraising departments within a particular organisation, then this needs to be stated to evaluation participants from the beginning, and consenting procedures need to outline possible future uses of the report (and provide opt-out clauses).

## *Dissemination*

Evaluation findings should be communicated effectively and appropriately to the relevant audiences. There are many ways to communicate and disseminate findings, and practitioners need to consider different possibilities right from the beginning. During the planning phase, therefore, in addition to thinking about how the final evaluation outputs will be used and by whom, different dissemination pathways should be considered, including conference presentations, journal articles, publicity flyers, DVDs, photographic exhibition and so on. The standard evaluation report, although most commonplace, is not the only form of dissemination.

## 1.2 Planning questions

Since many seemingly minor details have major consequences upon the evaluation design, process and outcomes, careful and responsible planning is non-negotiable. Many of these details depend on various combinations, ranging from the personal preferences of the evaluation commissioner, project focus, funding structures, time and skills available, and accessibility to evaluation participants.

A scheduled conversation with a strategic person (e.g. the manager or funder) will help address and clarify important details, and minimise wasted time, energy and hindrances later in the evaluation process. This will also help focus the evaluation and decrease the likelihood of collecting data and material that is not valuable or necessary to the evaluation.

Some planning questions are listed below:

- What is the overall aim of this evaluation?
- For whom and how will the evaluation outputs be helpful?
- What do practitioners need to know and why?
- What type of data and material will provide the best possible evidence?
- Whose voice would be the most representative?
- How many different people are likely to read the evaluation report?
- How much time does the audience have to read the report?
- What is the final submission deadline for the report?
- Are there any ethics review committees whose approval is needed before beginning data collection?
- Does the organisation have consent forms for the use of photographs and artwork? Do these forms cover the purposes of an evaluation report?
- Can service users and staff be approached for questionnaires and interviews?
- Are there any organisational politics behind the commissioning of this evaluation that it would be helpful to know about?
- This evaluation will take up X hours. Is there a budget for this time, and, if not, can the evaluation be scheduled as part of the existing hours funded?
- What evaluation outputs are required?

- Is a written evaluation report needed? If yes, what scale of evaluation report is required? How much detail? Is there a word limit?

- In what format should the report to be delivered? Hard copy or electronic? Do confidentiality agreements prohibit emailing of files with sensitive information?

- Who will need to check the first draft of the evaluation report?

- What is the 'language' or vocabulary of the target audience and organisation? What are their ethos and philosophy, their values and priorities? Do they rely upon 'buzz words' like 'impact', look for certain phrases or need to see medical terminology?

Although thinking ahead requires considerable effort, this helps to frame the right questions, helps to ensure focused, efficient data collection, and ensures that the right kind of output reaches the right kind of audience. Although some answers may be refined at a later stage, it is important to start exploring the right kind of questions at the planning phase. While planning, practitioners are encouraged to keep written records of the information they collect; any questions that may arise as part of this collecting procedure may be useful at later stages (e.g. report writing).

## 1.3 Developing a collaborative attitude

Evaluation is not a solo activity. As previously stated, evaluation requires input from a whole community within which different people undertake different roles. As part of mapping the resources (both material and human) available for the evaluation, it is worth considering existing networks both within and beyond the organisation. Local universities, external evaluation teams or experts within the community may well be available as resources to call on, to advise and to provide peer support.

Collaborative work between different arts therapists, arts & health practitioners as well as other professionals can be a refreshing experience right from the planning stages of an evaluation, offering unique opportunities to share learning, thinking, practices and skills. In her book *Arts Therapies in Schools*, dance movement therapist and researcher Vicky Karkou stresses the importance of interdisciplinary collaboration:

> Collaborations that 'work' have the potential to contribute towards cultural shifts that question the tradition of the sole practitioner who works on his or her own in the back room, the basement or the kitchen area, forgotten and disconnected from the rest of the school. Collaboration can enable arts therapists to bypass the fact that they are usually the only arts therapist employed in a particular setting, and create real or virtual links with other professionals. (Karkou, 2010, p.278)

A collaborative attitude, of course, is equally important in all contexts within which arts therapists and arts & health practitioners may find themselves working. Collaboration has the potential to generate or trigger certain 'cultural shifts' within the organisation. Although these shifts usually take time in order to flourish, it is crucial for their seeds to be in place right from the planning phase and throughout an evaluation project. Opportunities for collaboration, including peer support and sharing, may well emerge within a supervisory or advisory context, and where there are none, it may be helpful to create supportive and critical peer-review structures.

## 1.4 Considering types of data

### Primary and secondary data

*Primary data* refers to new information that is generated and collected for the purposes of an evaluation. The collection tools mentioned in this guide function usually as ways of generating 'primary data'.

*Secondary data* refers to pre-existing material. This includes information or material that has been collected previously for another purpose. When used for evaluation purposes, this material becomes classified as 'secondary data'. Such data may include information collected from practitioners' everyday practice notes, annual reports, video recordings, as well as organisational information such as demographics or a mission statement. The use of secondary data can impact positively on the cost and time resources of an evaluation project. It not only helps practitioners avoid collecting data that is already available, but also minimises evaluator and participant burden. Therefore, it is worth investing time and resources to investigate what data already exists and whether or not such data is relevant to the evaluation project. What is primary data for one evaluation could be used as secondary data for another evaluation. However, it is crucial to consider all ethical implications of using pre-existing material (Farrant, Pavlicevic and Tsiris, 2014).

Secondary data can be used either unprocessed (e.g. demographic figures) or processed. Case studies or vignettes are common examples of (processed) secondary data used in evaluation reports. The use of case studies is of particular relevance to arts therapists and arts & health practices, since it allows practitioners' voices and tacit knowledge to be communicated, and it helps to frame the evaluation findings with real-life, tangible examples (Higgins, 1993; Smeijsters and Aasgaard, 2005).

## Numbers and narratives

Data (irrespective of being primary or secondary) comes in a range of guises – it can be numeric, narrative, pictorial or audio; it can appear as charts or tables; it can be the result of complex computations, or a direct representation of a handwritten note.

Traditionally, the pros and cons of quantitative or qualitative data form part of a long-established debate as to which might be more robust and/or reliable. For practitioners undertaking evaluations, the best advice seems to be to consider what types of data will best address the purposes of the evaluation, rather than committing to either side of this long-standing debate (Tsiris and Hartley, 2013). Rather than being generated on the basis of the methodological debate, evaluation data needs to be fit-for-purpose. Health policy academic Norma Daykin writes:

> Nevertheless, there is still a debate about what constitutes robust evidence and within the broader arts for health field

there is an identified concern that too much emphasis on quantitative outcomes research may inhibit recognition of, or even damage, important arts processes. (Daykin, 2007, p.98)

While, at a broad-brush policy level, numeric data may indeed hold more weight within some quarters, at an evaluation level, practitioners need to focus on their evaluation aims and target audiences. These define the type of data to be generated, along with the resources of each evaluation context, as well as the nature of the service (Hedrick, 1994). A more contextual, pragmatic and functional attitude towards the choice of methods means that, for the purposes of arts therapy and arts & health service evaluations, a mixture of data types and methods is used.

Particular types of data are not necessarily linked to particular types of collection tools or methods. A questionnaire, for example, can collect numeric or narrative data depending on its design (as explained in Phase 2). Likewise, particular types of data are not necessarily linked to particular types of analysis. In other words, numeric data can be analysed using qualitative analysis methods (and therefore yield qualitative findings), and vice versa (as explained in Phase 4).

Although every audience will have their own preference – be it numeric, narrative, pictorial, or a mixture of all three – it is best to plan for the mixture of data types. This will represent a full and rounded picture of the service. Most important is to ensure that the chosen data collection methods are in harmony with the evaluation aims and objectives.

## 1.5 Considering supplementary evaluation material

In addition to considering the different types of primary and secondary data, practitioners are encouraged to plan for any supplementary material that may be useful for the evaluation outputs.

Supplementary material (such as photographs, audio and video recordings) can support, complement and illustrate the collected evaluation data. This is particularly helpful where the context and process of arts-based work is insufficiently represented through only words and numbers. Photographs, audio and video recordings can be a powerful means of bringing words and numbers to life. Such supplementary material can also be accessible to a wider audience, since it often requires minimal literacy skills to understand.

Collecting supplementary material is usually straightforward and cheap. Technology enables practitioners to use portable digital recording devices and cameras through which they can document people and places in action. Digital recordings are also easy to share and edit. However, practitioners need to be alert to the danger of ending up with a huge amount of material, which may result in a time-consuming editing procedure. Also, practitioners need to be alert to the ethical implications of taking photographs and recording people. Collecting supplementary material needs to be treated with ethical rigour, and the confidentiality and safe storage of such material is particularly important (for further information on ethics, see 'A Note on Ethics', page 161).

Practitioners' choice regarding the use of one or more types of supplementary material needs to be informed by the different possibilities and limitations of each type of material in relation to their own practice, organisational policies and desired evaluation outputs.

## 1.6 Considering data collection tools

Evaluations depend on assembling specific information from targeted sources in order to address particular questions. Many kinds of information contribute to an evaluation report and other outputs: from formal to ad hoc, from written to audio and pictorial, from 'formal' to 'informal', from pre-existing to specially gathered.

The gathering of data[6] is through the use of data collection tools or instruments, and since there are many different types of tools that collect different sorts of data, an essential part of planning involves staying aware and informed about various options, and making a decision as to what collection tools will be

---

6    This guide uses the umbrella term 'data', to signify information that is gathered and analysed systematically, for purposes of evaluation.

used for an evaluation project. Common evaluation instruments include questionnaires, interviews, focus groups, attendance log-sheets, reflective journals and observation guides (Figure 6).

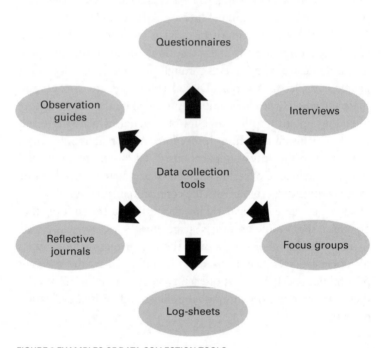

FIGURE 6 EXAMPLES OF DATA COLLECTION TOOLS

Practitioners usually need to develop collection tools according to the evaluation profile and work context, but in some cases existing tools can easily be adapted. Designing (or choosing) the right tool is crucial to ensuring that the evaluation captures the information needed (more about this in Phase 2). As previously mentioned, the choice or design of the evaluation tool depends on a range of factors, including respondents' age, mental capacity, literacy skills and availability. Such factors will determine the most sensitive and appropriate way to elicit information and therefore impacts the design of data collection tools.

Generally, a combination of different tools are needed to ensure that a broad and deep range of data is collected – while ensuring that the evaluation focus is retained. This process of generating (and combining) data from more than one data source or through more than one tool is known as 'triangulation' (Sale, Lohfeld and Brazil, 2002), which enhances the validity and trustworthiness of the evaluation findings. Of course, any triangulation process has to be scheduled right from the planning phase.

Inevitably, each data collection tool has advantages and disadvantages (Table 4). Instead of relying on the tools and methods that are most familiar, or that seem to be the 'easier' option, practitioners' choices need to be informed by each tool's possibilities and limitations. Ultimately, it is the kind of data needed that should dictate the choice of evaluation tool(s).

In addition to (or instead of) designing their own evaluation tool(s), practitioners may consider using tools designed and used by other people or organisations. Although this guide focuses on creating bespoke evaluation tools that are uniquely adapted for arts-based practices and projects, there are some existing, pre-designed tools that may be appropriate. Most of these tools have been developed for research purposes but can still be relevant in evaluation contexts. Some examples of such tools are the Outcomes Star, PSYCHLOPS, as well as some speech and language therapy tools.

**TABLE 4 Examples of data collection tools: possibilities, limitations and examples of use**

| Tools | Possibilities | Limitations | Examples of use |
|---|---|---|---|
| Questionnaires | • Can be completed in private and returned by post or filled in at an event or activity<br>• Can be completed in print or electronically (i.e. online questionnaire)<br>• Large numbers can be distributed<br>• Can be simple tick box in style, ask open questions or include rating scales<br>• Time-efficient<br>• Cost-effective<br>• Uniformity of data – easy to compile and analyse | • Often not completed or returned<br>• Sometimes reveal superficial (rather than in-depth) data<br>• Rely on written language comprehension and literacy skills, which may be inappropriate for some people<br>• The questions may 'pre-define' the responses if not carefully constructed<br>• Misinterpretation of questions<br>• No full answers; lack of rich narrative<br>• No guarantee of timely return | To collect participants':<br>• perceptions<br>• ratings<br>• opinions<br>• suggestions |
| Interviews | • Allow in-depth discussion<br>• Allow the interviewee's narratives and experiences to be explored, taking into account their personal context<br>• Good for getting detailed information about participants' opinions, feelings and ideas<br>• Can be conducted in private<br>• Allow flexibility – can be adapted according to interviewees' responses (i.e. semi-structured interviews) | • Time-consuming to carry out<br>• Some people may feel intimidated<br>• Interviewer may influence or 'lead' responses | To collect participants':<br>• in-depth personal accounts of experiences |

| | Advantages | Disadvantages | Purpose |
|---|---|---|---|
| Focus groups | • Group discussion can set off wide-ranging views and feedback<br>• Can be self-led<br>• Small groups of people can stimulate discussion and may help people to explore their experience of the service in more depth as they respond to others | • Can be difficult to arrange (finding suitable time and location for group members)<br>• The group formation is not necessarily 'representative' of the wider population (e.g. only the most confident may take part or contribute)<br>• Group dynamics can be difficult to overcome | To collect participants':<br>• in-depth personal accounts of experiences |
| Attendance log-sheets | • Allow systematic collation of numeric data (e.g. attendance numbers to sessions)<br>• Cost-effective<br>• Time-efficient<br>• Providing overview over a period of time | • Limited capacity for collecting of narrative data | To collect numbers of:<br>• sessions<br>• session attendances<br>• referrals<br>• cancellations |

*continued*

**TABLE 4 Examples of data collection tools: possibilities, limitations and examples of use** *continued*

| Tools | Possibilities | Limitations | Examples of use |
|---|---|---|---|
| Reflective journals | • Can provide documentation and evidence of change during activities for participants<br>• Simple<br>• Cost-effective<br>• Can be completed online<br>• Can trace short daily notes on the progress of a project<br>• Can note participants' feelings and opinions about a project | • Rely on literacy skills<br>• Journals may be seen as private, and participants may be unwilling to share contents<br>• Participants may present a falsely positive view<br>• Time-consuming data analysis process<br>• People may be reluctant to share what they have written, and prefer to keep journals private | To collect participants':<br><br>• personal accounts of experiences<br>• personal reflections during the process |
| Observation guides | • Help follow the progress of a small number of people experiencing a service<br>• Can give in-depth insight into people's experiences and interests<br>• Help gain insight into the experience as a whole, and for evaluating management and workshop skills<br>• Help capture contextual/environmental aspects of practice | • Time-consuming and labour-intensive<br>• People (participants/observants) may find it intrusive<br>• Can be difficult to observe a large group systematically (but following one or two people through a session or visit can be illuminating) | To collect participants':<br><br>• observations<br>• ad hoc accounts with people in-situ |

The Outcomes Star (www.outcomesstar.org.uk) is a suite of tools, adapted for different client groups and services, for supporting and measuring change when working with people. There are 15 versions of the Outcomes Star, including the Music Therapy Star which measures musical and interpersonal interaction. PSYCHLOPS (www.psychlops.org.uk) is an example of a short mental health outcome measure which can assess change during the course of psychotherapeutic interventions. Capturing data before, during and after a course of therapy, it elicits psychometric information covering three domains: problems, function and wellbeing. PSYCHLOPS Kids is a version for children aged 7–13 years.

Practitioners may also consider using existing tools from the field of speech and language therapy. Music therapist Felicity North (2011), for example, uses the Early Communication Assessment (Coupe O'Kane and Goldbart, 1998) which charts development from pre-intentional to intentional communication through observation of identified behaviours.

Although these examples refer to instruments which have been carefully designed and used in diverse settings and by a number of professionals, practitioners need to examine critically the suitability of such tools for the specific context and needs of their own evaluation. An existing tool is not necessarily a carefully designed tool. Also, practitioners are encouraged to consider the possibility of adapting an existing tool to suit their own evaluation needs and purposes. Music therapist Martin Lawes, for example, reports on how he adapted the AQR (Assessment of the Quality of Relationship) instrument (originally developed by Schumacher and Calvet, 2007) to evaluate and report on the outcomes of his music therapy work at a school for children with autism (Lawes, 2012).

Finally, practitioners need to keep in mind that existing tools may be expensive to purchase and training may be essential for the appropriate use of a tool. In any case, however, and irrespective of whether or not one chooses to use an existing tool, practitioners' knowledge of what already exists helps to inform their ways of gathering the right kind of data.

Although Phase 1 may seem unnecessarily detailed, this foundational information ensures that the evaluation process will be as efficient as possible. This is the kind of efficiency and representation that service users and evaluation participants deserve, and which arts-based services need in order to be portrayed robustly.

On the basis of the information collected in this phase, practitioners should have a clear picture of their project's evaluation framework, including their evaluation aims and objectives, the participants, the timeline, the data collection tools, the organisation's regulations and formalities, as well as their target audience and the kind of outputs that need to be produced at the end of the project. All this information (and the decisions made in Phase 1) will enable practitioners to move on to the next phase, which focuses on developing data collection tools.

# Phase 2

## Developing Data Collection Tools

Although Phase 2 encourages practitioners to design project-specific and service-specific data collection tools (also called instruments), even where external evaluators or organisations prefer to use their own tools, practitioners need to be familiar with the nuts and bolts of developing questionnaires, interview schedules, log-sheets and observation guides. Through familiarity with and a basic knowledge of data collection designs, practitioners are better positioned to critique other existing evaluation tools that may seem to have little to do with arts-based practices and the provision of relevant services – for example, condition-related outcome measures, organisational interview schedules, agency-designed survey questionnaires. A basic knowledge of evaluation tool design will also allow practitioners to consider adapting existing data collection tools and/or developing their own complementary tools. During early stages of developing data collection tools, a corresponding system, such as a blank data spreadsheet, needs to be designed in order that collected data (Phase 3) can be entered and analysed efficiently (Phase 4).

Once evaluation tools are designed, and have been tested with a pilot or trial run, the evaluation data collection phase is still not quite ready to begin. Before data can be collected, all necessary ethical considerations need to be in place, which may include the completion of participant information sheets and consent forms. However, host organisations will vary with regard to their policy on ethical review for evaluation projects (for more information about ethics, see 'A Note on Ethics', page 161).

## 2.1 Developing questionnaires

There are probably as many questionnaire designs as there are projects, organisations, practices and preferences. Questionnaires can be relatively easy to compile, brief for respondents to complete, and provide straightforward information. They can also be complex, asking for information in different ways and making increased demands on respondents' time.

Questionnaire design depends on the kind of data needed, which depends on the evaluation aims, the number of responses sought and the resources (including time and skills) available to the practitioner for processing questionnaire responses.

The phrasing, structure and layout of a questionnaire inevitably affects the way participants respond, the likelihood of their completing it and the richness and usefulness of the data collected. For example, some questions need yes/no or agree/disagree responses, whereas others can ask for statements to be rated, ranked or replaced; already these require different skill levels and commitment from respondents.

Some questions call for more 'open' responses; for example, questions beginning with 'Who', 'What', 'Why', 'Where', 'When' and 'How' cannot be answered with a simple 'yes' or 'no'. Other questions ask for written descriptions, drawings or other representations of value and experience. In some circumstances, respondents may be less likely to spend time answering more searching questions (or they may lack the resources and skills to do so) and find it easier to choose from a range of options or circle a score. A combination of scoring, tick boxes and open questions can be useful and reassuring to respondents, and effective in generating a range of data. Although narrative/pictorial data is more difficult to assemble and certainly more time-consuming to analyse, it may provide useful material for the evaluation outputs.

Since questionnaire response rates can be notoriously low, it may be worth the practitioner administering the questionnaire directly (i.e. by going through each question with the respondent face-to-face). On the other hand, it is crucial to ensure that enough questionnaires are circulated, to ensure a sufficient number of responses are gathered.

Guidelines for developing questionnaires are presented in some detail below. While running the risk of being over-inclusive and over-particular, the level of detail provided here helps to emphasise that formulating questions and designing questionnaires is a time-consuming minefield. Also, a poorly constructed questionnaire wastes people's time and almost guarantees that no satisfactory data will be collected.

### Keep it short

There are no universal agreements about the optimal length of a questionnaire. Short, simple questionnaires usually attract higher response rates than long, complex ones. Unsurprisingly, a survey of stroke survivors showed that both the response rate and the proportion of completed forms were significantly higher for a short 6-question form compared with a longer and more complex 36-question form (Dorman *et al.*, 1997).

When planning a questionnaire, it is useful to make a distinction between what is essential information, what would be useful and what is unnecessary information. Essential questions should be retained, while useful questions should be kept to a minimum, and superfluous questions should be discarded.

### Use simple words and sentences

The wording of questions needs to ensure that respondents will interpret or understand the questions in the same way. Since it is unlikely that everyone has the same understanding of the facts or a common basis of knowledge, even commonly used abbreviations or organisational jargon need to be explained.

Simple language helps to ensure, rather than assume, a common understanding, especially in circumstances where questionnaire respondents have diverse cultural backgrounds and literacy skills. Short, simple sentences are less confusing and less ambiguous than long, complex sentences. The clearest and most understandable sentences contain only one or two clauses. A question such as 'How do you feel on Wednesday and Sunday, after movement therapy in the afternoon?' can be interpreted ambiguously. A solution would be to break it into two more specific and separate questions: 'How do you feel after movement therapy on Wednesday afternoons?' and 'How do you feel after movement therapy on Sunday afternoons?'

### Avoid difficult or unfamiliar concepts

Many respondents may well be unfamiliar with practice-specific or site-specific terms. For example, asking family members of people with dementia the question 'Do you agree with the statements in the new National Dementia Strategy?' assumes that all family members are well informed and stay regularly up to date with government strategy.

### Ask for only one piece of information at a time

For example, 'Are the poetry sessions at a convenient time and place?' [Yes/No] asks for two pieces of information at the same time. It should be divided into two parts: 'Are the poetry sessions (a) at a convenient time [Yes/No], (b) at a convenient place?' [Yes/ No]

### Ask precise questions

Questions may be ambiguous if a word or term has more than one meaning; medicine, for example, could be interpreted as the general practice of medicine or as actual medication. Equally, phrasing can be ambiguous – for example, 'What do they do in music therapy sessions?' Precision prevents misunderstandings.

### Consider the level of detail needed

Questionnaire respondents need guidance as to the amount and level of detail required in the response. Since an open question can be answered in a sentence or in a full page of text, it is helpful to direct the respondents – for example, by instructing 'In two or three sentences, describe...'

## Consider the order of questions

Since the evaluator wants to ensure respondents' optimal and sustained engagement with the questionnaire in order to elicit as rich and accurate a body of information as possible, the clustering and sequencing of questionnaire questions is a highly strategic exercise. Starting the questionnaire with questions that are likely to be easy and quick to answer, which sound interesting and attract respondents' attention, enables them to feel engaged and comfortable. Questions that might be perceived as complex or threatening to some, or call for further thought, are best positioned later in the questionnaire; otherwise, these questions may result in loss of confidence and an incomplete questionnaire.

The information elicited in any one question inevitably influences how subsequent questions are read and answered. Some suggestions include:

- progressing from general to specific questions, from easy to difficult, from factual to subjective/personal

- starting with closed format questions and questions that are directly relevant to the main subject

- questions that elicit demographic and personal information (e.g. sex, age, cultural background, professional title) can be placed towards the end as they may influence the spontaneity of respondents' engagement with the rest of the questions.

## Ask questions in the right way

Since many people answer questions in a way they perceive to be socially desired or anticipated by the questioner, they often look for clues in the questions. Many apparently neutral questions can potentially be biased. For example, in the question 'Within the past month, how many art therapy sessions have you missed due to time management?' participants may perceive the desired responses to be 'never'. This question could be rephrased as 'Within the past month, on how many occasions did other scheduled meetings did not allow you to attend art therapy sessions?'

## Avoid leading questions

Leading questions demand a specific response and do not leave space for disagreement. They are not considered to be good practice and can compromise the integrity of an evaluation by inviting skewed responses. For example, the question 'Do you agree that group arts interventions are extremely powerful in helping this client group?' leads participants to feel as though they must agree with the statement.

## Avoid double negatives

Questions using two negatives together take time to decipher and are best avoided; for example, 'Why wouldn't you not want to miss a music improvisation class?'

## Ensure positive and negative statements

Arts therapy and arts & health practices may have positive and/or negative impact. Not exploring the latter has often been criticised (Gold *et al.*, 2013). Questionnaires need to include both positive and negative options, particularly in checklist questions, and should provide space for respondents to air any negative comments. This helps to avoid skewed or biased findings, which ensures the reliability and integrity of an evaluation design.

## Balance opinion/attitudes rating scales

When respondents are being asked to rate their opinion/attitude (e.g. in a Likert scale), the scale needs to cover opposite extremes – for example, *Strongly Disagree, Disagree, Neutral, Agree* and *Strongly Agree* should all appear together.

## Keep checklists short

Checklists are best kept short – a maximum of ten items/options is recommended. This helps to keep respondents engaged and prevents questionnaire fatigue.

### *Frame sensitive issues carefully*

It is often difficult to obtain truthful answers to sensitive questions. What constitutes a sensitive question depends on the service, the evaluation participant, the timing of the evaluation, and organisational politics.

The guide has already hinted that developing a questionnaire needs nuanced planning for all kinds of reasons – some of which are more subtle than others. Since there are many types of data (with implications for data collecting, storing and processing), questionnaire design also needs to consider what questions to ask in order to obtain the responses that will provide the right kind of data to address evaluation aims.

## 2.2 Formulating questions (and answers)

As stated earlier, a combination of different kinds of questions helps to keep the respondents' attention and engages their interest. Here, questions are categorised as either open-ended or closed. One consideration in formulating questionnaires is to use a combination of closed and open-ended questions.

### *Open-ended questions*

An open-ended question seeks a descriptive response: respondents are invited to answer in their own words and as elaborately or minimally as they wish. At risk of oversimplifying, open-ended questions tend to seek the 'hows' and the 'whys', rather than the 'yesses' or 'noes'. They are useful for eliciting a comprehensive range of descriptions and generally provide rich, detailed and personal answers. However, an excessive number of open-ended questions risks reducing the quality of the attention the respondents give to the answers (which are likely to become more and more brief as the questionnaire goes on) and can also result in an enormous amount of data.

### *Closed questions*

Closed questions generally ask respondents to choose from a limited set of answers, and can be quick and easy to complete.

They provide a fixed number of responses, which lend themselves well to numeric representation and analysis (see Phase 4).

Since closed questions use a number of methods for collecting answers, some that are commonly useful to arts-based practitioners are presented below.

### 'YES' OR 'NO' (OR 'NOT SURE')

This is the simplest form of answer, and although this question type has its limitations, it is valuable when used appropriately; questions requiring 'Yes', 'No' or 'Not sure' answers can contribute to reporting percentages in the final report. For example, 'In total, 98% of participants want the drama sessions to continue.' Strong statements such as these add clarity and a persuasive edge to evaluation outputs which funding may rely upon. Importantly, providing a neutral 'Not sure' option (in addition to 'Yes' and 'No' options) is a good practice.

### TICK BOXES

Tick box options are useful for specifying and directing the respondent to the type of information needed. However, tick boxes need to provide the respondent with both positive and negative options (as equally weighted as possible), without which the evaluation findings are skewed. It is also important to provide an 'other' box with space for the participant to voice any options they feel have not been mentioned. As already stated, providing too many options can cause participants questionnaire fatigue; it is therefore advisable to keep a small number of options, and phrase each option in a concise manner.

Specifying how many boxes respondents need to tick (i.e. 'Tick as many as apply' or 'Tick one box only') is a good practice. For example:

> **What is your position at Longview Community Centre?'** *(Tick one box only)*
> ☐ Service user
> ☐ Management staff member
> ☐ Parent/guardian of service user
> ☐ Care staff team member
> ☐ Other (please specify: _____ )

If including a question that provides numerical ranges, the options need to allow for every value possible. For example:

**How long have you worked at Longview?** *(Tick one box only)*

☐ less than 1 year ☐ 1–2 years

☐ 3–4 years ☐ 5 or more years

## RANKING

Ranking is slightly more complicated than being provided with a set of tick box options. With ranking, the respondent is invited to rank the options in terms of priority or relevance. These graded responses may provide more enlightening evaluation outcomes than a simple tick-box question. For example:

**Please rank your interests in the following...** *(Please order the items according to the following scale; 1 = most important to 8 = least important)*

☐ singing ☐ playing music with other people

☐ drumming ☐ listening to music

☐ playing in a band ☐ talking about music

☐ going to concerts ☐ moving to music

It may be simpler to switch the numbers around – that is, request that respondents rank 8 as the most important and 1 as the least important. This will allow for greater simplicity when analysing and totalling the responses (i.e. largest score/total reflects higher importance).

## LIKERT SCALE

The Likert scale (as well as the semantic differential scale explained below) is useful for considering respondents' attitudes or opinions. The Likert scale asks respondents to agree or disagree along a scale of options, with a series of statements. As well as providing opposing statements, so that respondents are unlikely to agree with everything, a 'neutral' option such as 'neither agree nor disagree' (or 'not sure') prevents respondents being forced towards false statements. For example:

---

**Drawing helps me express my feelings.** *(Please tick one)*
☐ Strongly disagree
☐ Disagree
☐ Neither agree nor disagree
☐ Agree
☐ Strongly agree

---

However, the 'neutral' option can be perceived as an easy option to take when a respondent is unsure; whether this option is a truly 'neutral' or 'undecided' option is questionable (Armstrong, 1987). Placing this option at either end of the scale or removing it completely (a method known as 'forced choice') are some ways of overcoming these kinds of problems. For example:

---

**Drawing helps me express my feelings.** *(Please tick one)*
☐ Strongly disagree
☐ Disagree
☐ Agree
☐ Strongly agree
☐ Neither agree nor disagree

---

## SEMANTIC DIFFERENTIAL

The semantic differential, one of the most widely used scales for the measurement of attitudes, invites respondents to place their mark on a line between two polar opposite adjectives (e.g. inadequate–adequate; worthless–valuable; weak–strong). The commonly used Visual Analogue Scale (VAS) uses the semantic differential method. When designing the scale, it is best not to have demarcations (e.g. for each centimetre), since respondents will be tempted to put across or a mark on the demarcation. A straight line allows for a more spontaneous and flexible response. For example:

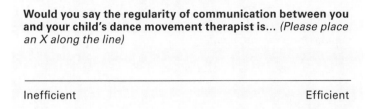

**Would you say the regularity of communication between you and your child's dance movement therapist is...** *(Please place an X along the line)*

Inefficient         Efficient

Another option is to use a numbering system (instead of a line). In this case each rating point should not be labelled with an individual descriptive (as it would be the case in a Likert scale). Usually, semantic differential scales are segmented with five or seven divisions between each pair of contrasting adjectives. For example:

**Would you say the efficiency of communication between you and your child's dance movement therapist is...** *(Please circle one number)*

| 1 | 2 | 3 | 4 | 5 |
|---|---|---|---|---|

Inefficient         Efficient

Sometimes the middle position of the scale can be used as a 'neutral' point, and therefore marked as '0'. For example:

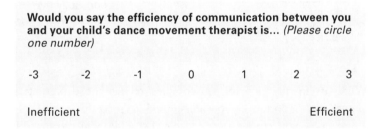

**Would you say the efficiency of communication between you and your child's dance movement therapist is...** *(Please circle one number)*

| -3 | -2 | -1 | 0 | 1 | 2 | 3 |
|----|----|----|---|---|---|---|

Inefficient         Efficient

Finally, a series of semantic differential scales placed one after the other can be used to rate a range of aspects. For example:

**Drawing from your experience of bringing your child to music therapy, please rate each of the following...** *(Please circle one number for each statement)*

| -3 | -2 | -1 | 0 | 1 | 2 | 3 |
|----|----|----|---|---|---|---|

The waiting area of the building **is not** welcoming

The waiting area of the building **is** welcoming

| -3 | -2 | -1 | 0 | 1 | 2 | 3 |
|----|----|----|---|---|---|---|

My child **is not** keen to come to music therapy

My child **is** keen to come to music therapy

| -3 | -2 | -1 | 0 | 1 | 2 | 3 |
|----|----|----|---|---|---|---|

I **do not** receive enough information about my child's music therapy

I **do** receive enough information about my child's music therapy

| -3 | -2 | -1 | 0 | 1 | 2 | 3 |
|----|----|----|---|---|---|---|

I **do not** value the music therapy service

I **do** value the music therapy service

When using any type of closed question (as those presented above), it is important to consider providing space for comments. Comments on the ratings given can elicit key additional information that cannot be captured through a rating scale alone.

## 2.3 Questionnaires and capacities

Questionnaires, like all evaluation tools, need to be user-friendly and accessible in order to ensure that the best possible information is collected efficiently. Questionnaire design needs to take into account the nature of the project, the age of the participants involved, their capacities and needs, their language and cultural background, and so on. Language is both a minefield and a goldmine. Overall, the best information is elicited when questionnaires are designed with the participants in mind, so that when it comes to completing it or having someone administer it, there are minimal obstacles to be overcome in order to make sense of the questions.

### *Questionnaires for children*

Depending on the children's age, an appropriate balance of simplicity and complexity ensures their interested engagement. Visuals and the use of colour can help make questionnaires exciting and fun, rather than a chore that reminds them of school work!

Language needs to be straightforward and familiar, with turns of phrase that they are likely to relate to. Questions such as 'What is your favourite activity in music classes?' could work well with young children, since talking about 'favourite things' (e.g. 'favourite colour' or 'favourite food') is a common interest with younger children, but possibly not with older children. Words and language in general have distinctive meanings at different stages of life, and it is important to be aware of words that children may not interpret in the same way as an adult would.

### *Questionnaires for people with learning disabilities*

Questionnaire design for people with learning disabilities needs to consider their unique profile, including mental/intellectual, language, visual and fine motor capacities. Generally, it is important that the questionnaire is visually clear with a lot of space and that it involves colour. Questions should be simple, practical and to the point, and relate directly to respondents' experiences. Likewise, language needs to be familiar, with words that are in everyday use. Keeping the questionnaire short also helps ensure optimal attention and engagement.

Where appropriate, symbols, images or other visual cues can be used to enhance engagement and understanding of questionnaires. Some people with learning disabilities may already use a particular communication system that involves visual cues (e.g. the Picture Exchange Communication System, known as PECS); in such cases, using visual cues in the questionnaire that are familiar to the respondents will aid their understanding and engagement.

Although some people with learning disabilities may not physically fill in a form themselves, the questionnaire can be used as a visual aid and a way of focusing them on the task at hand.

### Questionnaires for staff

The expertise of staff members is their inside knowledge of an organisation, their practical experience and personal relationships with service users. Staff are often a rich source of contextual examples and anecdotes, which can provide valuable evaluation material. Staff can provide rich information about everyday organisational life, the service within its organisational context and people's engagement with the service. Questionnaires need to be short since busy staff members are unlikely to spend a significant amount of time completing them. Also, the language needs to be suitable for a range of people; it is important not to assume total literacy or familiarity with the English language.

### Questionnaires for family members, practitioners, visitors...and anyone else

All points made above apply to other groups of people, who can be from any social context or country. Targeted, tailored, accessible and interesting questionnaires, which ask pertinent questions in the right way, guarantee the best and most efficient responses.

Often feedback can be helpful even if some respondents (such as family members) may have only 'indirect' experience of the service. A wife of a mental health patient, for example, may have never attended a music therapy session, but she may often talk to her husband about his music therapy experiences. Her feedback about the service may be invaluable.

## 2.4 Questionnaires for pre–post comparison

Services or projects with a fixed start and end date can benefit from a pre- and post- comparison by handing out questionnaires before the project has started, then again at the end of the project. Pre–post questionnaires can provide a systematic comparison of change and development that has taken place over the course of the project or service. Attention is needed to avoid making quick assumptions and attributing changes, whether positive or negative, directly to the service, since this leads to simplistic and inaccurate cause-and-effect explanations. Instead, the provision of concurrent services and external influences need to be acknowledged, so that change is not inaccurately accredited solely to the service or project.

Pre- and post-questionnaires usually ask the same questions so that they are directly comparable, and here numeric data becomes particularly important and useful. One suitable method is the semantic differential; where the respondent rates their opinion on a scale from one extreme to another, and two sets of scores (pre and post) can be compiled for the same scale. For example, in the context of a project that has the aim of increasing the flexibility of physically disabled children, parents may be asked the following:

**Pre-project questionnaire 1**

**Please rate your child's current range of movement in general.** *(Please circle one number)*

1          2          ③          4          5

Inflexible                                              Flexible
movement                                              movement

**Please comment upon your rating.**

_____

_____

**Post-project questionnaire 1**

**Please rate your child's current range of movement in general.** *(Please circle one number.)*

1          2          3          ④          5

Inflexible                                              Flexible
movement                                              movement

**Please comment upon your rating.**

_____

_____

## 2.5 Surveys

The advantage of surveys, especially when administered electronically, is that a substantial number of respondents can be approached and a significant amount of data collected. Data collection of this scale can be a complex enterprise, and large-scale surveys are predominantly conducted by experts in the field of evaluation. Since large-scale surveys are an unlikely evaluation design for arts-based practitioners who are evaluating predominantly small-scale practices, only general points are considered here.

The best surveys are well structured and engaging, and call for different kinds of information (e.g. numeric and narrative) through a variety of approaches, including open-ended and closed questions, Likert scales, semantic differential scales, checklists and rankings. Efficient structuring and preparation is crucial.

### Naming the survey when distributing electronically

Since many people discard electronic messages simply on the basis of their subject or the identity of the sender, it is well worth carefully considering what titles are likely to attract the interest of the recipients.

### Covering letter

A personalised covering letter of invitation that includes an introduction explaining briefly the purpose of the survey signals respect and professionalism; however, the letter should in no way be coercive. Covering letters often serve as participant information sheets (PIS) and consent forms at the same time (for further information on PIS and consent forms, see 'A Note on Ethics', page 161). Finally, it is always advisable to thank the respondent at the end of surveys.

## 2.6 Developing interview schedules

Interviews are a good way to elicit detailed and relevant information that provides a rich narrative source of opinions, feelings and ideas. Interviews are usually done on a one-to-one basis or in groups – generally known as 'focus groups'. Whether for individual or group interviews, questions need to be planned in advance with prompts and probes to help ensure that all necessary information is gathered. The same or similar questions should be asked of each interviewee to ensure consistency of information that will help draw together data for analysis when many people have been interviewed. Interviews can be structured, semi-structured or unstructured, allowing different degrees of flexibility. One-to-one interviews with children, young people and vulnerable adults can be complex due to safeguarding issues; the presence of a carer or authorised adult is strongly recommended in such cases. In some cases, a carer or designated person can carry out and record the interview on behalf of the evaluator.

Interviews with small groups of people (i.e. focus groups) can stimulate discussion and encourage people to explore their experience of the service in more depth as they respond to comments by others. A prepared, pre-tested interview schedule helps to keep the discussion focused. Small group discussions can also be self-led, with the group being provided with the interview schedule; the evaluator does not need to be present if interviewees are able to keep the discussion going without assistance. There are both advantages and disadvantages to using this approach.

Interviews usually require a flexible structure; however, there are certain principles and techniques that are applicable to most interviews. Interview schedules should be structured into three main sections: the opening, the main body of questions and the closing.

### *Opening*

The opening to an interview should always make the interviewee feel welcome and relaxed through establishing a rapport. In addition, the opening should clearly indicate the purpose of the interview and make it clear what subject areas will be discussed, so that interviewees know where the conversation is going. Providing a context for the evaluation, and an explanation for how the information discussed will be valuable, helps to motivate the respondent(s) to answer questions fully and in a relevant way. It is important to indicate from the start the amount of time the interview is expected to take and, finally, to check that respondents are happy to be recorded and for notes to be made during the interview, with reassurance that all information they divulge will be kept confidential and their identity will remain anonymous.

**Establish a rapport**

My name is [*your name*] and I thought it would be great to speak with you about your experiences of the Music Therapy Project at Light House.

**Purpose and structure**

I would like to ask you some questions, first, about your condition, then about your previous experiences in a medical setting, your experiences of the project and what you feel the impact of this project has been over the past few months.

**Motivation**

Your responses will help us to know how to make the project even better for next year, so that people like you can have the best possible experience on the project.

**Time**

This interview should take about ten minutes in total.

**Consent**

Are you happy with me recording the interview and taking brief notes while we speak? Anything you say will be kept confidential and your identity will be kept anonymous.

FIGURE 7 EXAMPLE OF INTERVIEW OPENING

## *The main body*

The main body of an interview schedule provides an overview of the topics to be covered and the potential questions, prompts and probes. The number of questions and the exact wording of the questions depend on the type of interview schedule used. The interview may be non-structured with only the topics and subtopics listed. A non-structured interview generally leaves out potential probing questions to allow the interviewer to adapt to the interaction that unfolds. However, the non-structured interview requires a highly skilled and experienced interviewer;

most interviewers rely on a semi-structured scheduled interview that contains main questions and possible prompts and probes to help the interviewee give more specific answers. This schedule still allows some freedom to probe into answers and adapt to the interview situation. In addition, the semi-structured schedule aids in recording answers and is easier to conduct. The order of questions in an interview is crucial to the interview's efficacy, just as in questionnaire planning and design.

Here are some tips for effective interview questions:

- Use warm-up questions at the start of the interview to help the interviewee feel more comfortable. This way they will relax more quickly and be able to have more elucidating insights, providing richer evaluation data.

- Questions should encourage discussion. Open-ended questions are preferred as they can provoke richer, more explorative and detailed answers. Open-ended questions often start with 'how', 'why' or 'what'. Although closed questions provide one-word answers, they are good for eliciting demographic information and at times can be used in conjunction with open-ended questions.

- The phrases 'Tell me about…' or 'Give me an example of…' help interviewees to engage with practical examples of certain situations. These little stories, accounts or vignettes provide particularly rich narrative data, which can help to capture the heart of someone's experience. Starting a questionnaire with one of these phrases helps to avoid unspecific or rambling discussions which do not get to the heart of what is happening in the service.

- Developing prompts and probes before the interview helps to keep the conversation in focus. Interviewees may not automatically give as much detail as required, or may provide too much information and go 'off track'. Prompts are questions that help interviewees to continue speaking about a more specific subject, while probes are questions that encourage interviewees to think more deeply about a subject. Used together, they help to steer interviewees in the right direction, while still ensuring that spontaneous and rich information is gathered. For example, a prompt and probe for a very general question such as 'How did participating in the theatre production impact your son?' could include 'What did you notice about your son's interaction with other people?'

- Avoid asking the same question twice (unless one deliberately wants to cross-check a piece of information from different angles). It is very easy to ask questions that sound different but provoke almost identical answers. Rather, questions need to be different in order to cover the full range of information needed.

- At times the interviewee may hesitate to express a strong opinion. In such cases, and if appropriate, interviewers can offer a deliberately strong, biased and perhaps controversial statement and invite the interviewee to either agree or disagree. For example, 'Tell me what you think about this statement: "Music therapy is a useless intervention for people with neurological impairments."' This technique (inspired by the Likert method) helps to signal to the interviewee that strong opinions are welcome, as are their feelings about situations and events.

- Questions need to be phrased in clear, colloquial language, rather than in a formal written style, which sounds stilted when it is read aloud.

- Jargon should be kept to a minimum in order to ensure that language is accessible, understandable and familiar for the interviewee.

## *Closing*

The closing part of the interview should be brief but not abrupt. The interviewer can forewarn the interviewee that they are approaching the end of the interview (e.g. before they ask the last or the penultimate question). At the end, interviewees should be asked if there is anything else they would like to add and if they have any questions. The closing also informs the interviewee about the next course of action to be taken, and, finally, the interviewer must maintain the rapport with the interviewee by thanking them for their time.

## A final note regarding layout of the interview schedule

Some interviewees may feel uncomfortable with being recorded and consequently will not give their consent. Recording an interview is helpful but not essential. If recording is not an option, it is helpful to prepare an annotation sheet that provides space to write down detailed notes for each question asked (Figure 8). Without this structure, it can be extremely difficult to determine which response belonged to which question.

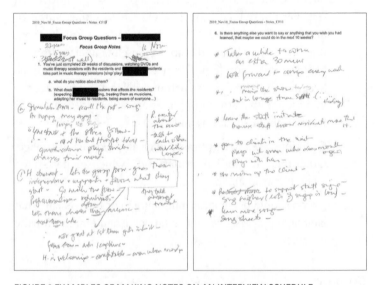

FIGURE 8 EXAMPLES OF MAKING NOTES ON AN INTERVIEW SCHEDULE

## 2.7 Developing log-sheets

A log-sheet is a collection tool for gathering data regularly and systematically, through a pre-designed chart. It provides a written record of the details of a service that are often, but not always, numeric. Log-sheets could include information such as the number of service users seen in one session, the number of sessions happening in a day, the number of new referrals, the number of staff in attendance, the conditions of service users and so on.

A log-sheet is useful for tracking information over time. Creating a log-sheet is relatively straightforward; with the design accommodating the information needed. Templates are often provided in spreadsheet and word processing programs, which can be easily customised for most situations.

There are a few aspects to consider when designing log-sheets:

- What information is needed altogether?

- How much information is needed at a time?

- Over how many weeks or months will the log-sheet be used?

- Will the collected information be entered directly into a computer? Or to a hard copy document and then transferred manually?

## *What information should a log-sheet include?*

Log-sheets can hold a range of types of information, and the temptation is to be over-inclusive rather than focused, especially since they are straightforward to design. However, simplicity is always the most effective and efficient use of a log-sheet. Although usually targeting numeric data, space can be created for narrative comments, anecdotal information and notes that explain aspects of the numeric data.

Information that is often collected in a log-sheet includes:

- the total number of service users attending any one session

- the number of service users attending over an entire day/ week

- the number of new referrals

- the profiles of service users (e.g. cultural background, conditions, needs, skills, age/gender)

- the number of staff, families or other people accessing the service

- the number of sessions or activities that take place in one day/week, and their different formats (e.g. individual, group or family sessions)

- the number of cancelled sessions or activities.

However, the data collected in a log-sheet should depend upon what is relevant for the purposes of the specific evaluation. Collecting a lot of information in a log-sheet is time-consuming and will be more complex to analyse later in the evaluation process.

### How to create a log-sheet?

Log-sheets are usually created using a spreadsheet that allows for numeric information to be easily entered and processed. One log-sheet can be used for a long period of time, collecting basic information and tracking how that information may change or develop. The different dates are usually pre-entered in the left hand column, while the type of the information to be collected is stated in the top row. The relevant data is then entered accordingly and a total for each column and row can be tallied. Figure 9 shows an example of a typical attendance log-sheet.

In evaluation projects where detailed information about service user or client groups is required, attendance log-sheets can be more complex. If developed for other practitioners to use, including brief usage guidelines may be helpful and will ensure consistency throughout the completion of the log-sheet (see, for example, Figure 10).

| Dates | Individual sessions | | | Group sessions | | | | Notes: who did a new referral, referral reason, reason for cancellation, etc. |
|---|---|---|---|---|---|---|---|---|
| | Number of clients attended | Number of new clients | Number of clients cancelled | Number of group sessions | Number of clients attended | Number of new clients | Number of group sessions cancelled | |
| 01.03.2013 | 4 | 1 | 0 | 2 | 9 | 2 | 0 | New individual and group clients referred by head nurse |
| 08.03.2013 | 3 | 0 | 1 | 2 | 10 | 1 | 0 | Client cancelled due to clashing hospital appointment |
| 15.03.2013 | 4 | 0 | 0 | 1 | 5 | 0 | 1 | 2nd group session cancelled due to class trip |
| | | | | | | | | |
| | | | | | | | | |

FIGURE 9 EXAMPLE OF A COMPLETED TYPICAL LOG-SHEET

## Music Therapy Attendance Log-Sheet

Clients are organised into the following categories: **a** = Autistic Spectrum Disorder; **b** = Challenging Behaviour; **c** = Hearing Impairment; **d** = Visual Impairment.

The attendance log-sheet is divided into four main sections:

**Individual Music Therapy** = Music therapy sessions with one client (with or without additional staff or other people). Please also note which category the clients belong to.

**Group Music Therapy** = Music therapy sessions with two clients or more (and additional staff or other people). Please also note which category the clients in each group belong to.

**New referrals** = Please write the total number of new music therapy referrals received on each day (sessions may not have started yet).

**Comments** = Please make a note of any anecdotal feedback you have had (e.g. quotes from clients, staff, etc.) that could be useful for the evaluation. Also, please provide any other information you think relevant (i.e. explain any significant variations in attendance numbers).

| Date | Individual Music Therapy | | | | | | | | Group Music Therapy | | | | | | | | | New Referrals | Comments |
| | Total no. of individual sessions | No. of clients per category | | | | Total no. of: | | | Total no. of group sessions | Total no. of clients per group | No. of clients per category | | | | Total no. of: | | | Total no. of new referrals | |
| | | a | b | c | d | Staff | Other | | | | a | b | c | d | Staff | Other | | | |
| | | | | | | | | | | | | | | | | | | | | |
| | | | | | | | | | | | | | | | | | | | | |
| | | | | | | | | | | | | | | | | | | | | |

FIGURE 10 EXAMPLE OF A COMPLEX LOG-SHEET

## 2.8 Developing reflective journals

Reflective journals can be an invaluable supportive source of information in an evaluation project. They can be used by project leaders and participants, including practitioners, service users and staff members – any evaluation participant. A predesigned, structured, reflective journal ensures that information is collected systematically. For example, including headings such as 'high points' and 'low points' helps to provide more focused information.

Reflective journals encourage participants to make daily notes and keep a record of their experiences, feelings and opinions in relation to the service. However, from the data analysis perspective, reflective journals can generate an enormous amount of data that is difficult to analyse and may not all be relevant to the evaluation aims. To avoid unnecessarily accumulating a huge amount of data, practitioners can employ a number of techniques. The journal's pages, for example, can be clearly segmented in a set of sub-sections each of which is assigned to each session; this way, participants have clearly defined space within which to write their comments and reflections on individual sessions.

Since some people may be reluctant to share what they have written in their journals and prefer to keep them private, confidentiality, privacy and anonymity issues need to be in place and clearly communicated to all participants right from the beginning.

## 2.9 Developing observation guides

Evaluative observation means watching an event with purpose, or through a particular frame, and making note of particular moments that are directly relevant to the evaluation aims. Not everything can be seen and absorbed at once, especially where the event being observed is large-scale (such as a performance) or in an open public space. In order to ensure focused information, observation guides help structure the exercise. Ideally, the observer should be not only someone who has the skill and dedication to undertake this task, but also someone who can be trusted by the practitioner and by those taking part – especially within a small-scale, intimate context. Observers can give useful feedback to an artist or workshop leader, as well as to participants during the project.

An observation guide needs to clearly signal what kind of information needs to be collected, always in relation to the specific evaluation aims. Examples of information that might be worth noting in an observation guide include physical and spatial arrangements, interactions between people and nonverbal behaviour, etc. (see Figure 11).

An observation guide should leave plenty of space to write freely and should include pointers for key information. Similar to reflective journals, however, observation guides can generate an unnecessarily large amount of data which may be unrealistic in terms of data analysis. Therefore practitioners need to specify from the beginning the type of information they need to collect and structure the observation guide accordingly.

## 2.10 Trialling data collection tools

Once the evaluation tools are designed and ready for use, they need to be trialled, preferably with more than one person and ideally with people who have different experiences, levels of participation, skills and roles. The trialling step is a crucial part of designing data collection tools, since it helps to ensure that these are accessible, clear and efficient, or, in other words, fit-for-purpose. Trialling tools provides opportunity for identifying potential gaps, formatting improvements and inconsistencies, identifying ambiguities, levels of engagement and areas of repetition before data collection begins. However, the scale and complexity of any trialling needs to be adapted according to the scale and complexity of each evaluation project. For small evaluation projects, simply asking a colleague to trial the evaluation tools could be adequate.

## OBSERVATION GUIDE

Name of observer:                    Date:

Event:                               Location:

Number of service users present:

| General | Yes | No | Comments and details |
|---|---|---|---|
| Does the session structure allow for broad group input? | | | |
| Is the space comfortable and well lit? | | | |
| Do service users feel comfortable in the space? | | | |
| Are the walls or space decorated in any way? | | | |
| **Qualities of interaction** | | | |
| All service users participate in the session. | | | |
| Body language of service users seems engaged and energised. | | | |
| Participation crosses racial, cultural, and gender boundaries. | | | |

Describe an interesting comment or exchange that occurred during the observation:

Any other comments:

Reminders for next week's observation:

FIGURE 11 EXAMPLE OF AN OBSERVATION GUIDE

In the case of large evaluation studies, it is worth considering the possibility of running a pilot project. In this case, one would go through the whole evaluation process but with only a small number of participants. At the end of the process, an assessment of what worked well and what did not work well needs to be conducted. On the basis of this assessment, relevant amendments can be made to improve the evaluation process for the main study. Although piloting may be time-consuming, it is worth doing for large evaluation projects or for projects where practitioners may feel unsure about the methodology.

Phase 2 is now complete – bearing in mind that there is always room for refining evaluation tools and adapting them according to the nature of specific evaluation projects. Phase 3 considers different aspects and issues that practitioners need to bear in mind while collecting the evaluation data and supplementary material.

# Phase 3

## Collecting Data and Supplementary Material

Once evaluation collection tools have been developed and tested in a trial or pilot run, they are ready for use – to collect data and supplementary material. This phase is crucial for the evaluation, and its success will depend not only on well-designed and tested tools but also on the time spent on approaching potential evaluation participants. Without due preparation, the collection phase can be demanding, since gaining access to service users and staff, particularly in hospital contexts, is often far more complicated than first anticipated. Additionally, before collecting data and material, participants need to be informed about the evaluation and provide their informed consent to participate (see 'A Note on Ethics', page 161).

Given the effort involved in designing and testing tools, it is worth everyone involved being as thoroughly prepared as possible to ensure that data and material are gathered systematically, efficiently and ethically. Phase 3 considers three main aspects that need to be kept in mind while collecting data:

- how to administer different collection tools
- how to identify the 'right' time and the 'right' participants
- how to create an evaluation community and shared ownership.

## 3.1 Administering different collection tools

Strategic planning is required for administering various collection tools. Depending on the evaluation framework, more than one collection tool may need to be administered during the same period of time. It is therefore necessary to ensure that a protocol is in place for storing and filing the various data and material as they are collected. This protocol could simply be a locked cabinet dedicated solely to completed questionnaires and other printed material, and/or a designated electronic folder, which is password-protected.

At all times, courtesy and respect are key, since participants are giving up their time and resources for the benefit of the evaluation. Remembering to thank them for their time and energy is easily forgotten throughout the lengthy evaluation process. In addition, even though participants will have already given informed consent (see 'A Note on Ethics', page 161), it is useful to remind them that their answers remain confidential. These details help to increase the likelihood of participants feeling engaged and offering as much useful information as they can.

### Collecting questionnaires

Questionnaires can be filled in either independently by the respondent (i.e. self-administration) or by a facilitator assisting the respondent. Since the mode of administration may affect the rate of participation as well as the accuracy and fullness of responses, the choice of administration method needs to be considered from the very beginning of the evaluation. The method will depend on a range of factors, including the number of respondents, their age, capacities and literacy skills, and the amount of time available for data collection.

Self-administered questionnaires are cost-effective and provide more privacy for the participants. However, they require thorough testing ahead of distribution because they provide limited control of whether or not the individual will interpret the questions as intended, and whether or not the individual will (fully or partly) complete and return the questionnaire. In Section 2.3, 'Questionnaires and capacities' (page 83), the implications of designing questionnaires for different populations (such as children and people with a learning disability) are considered. Each of the groups considered will need a particular approach in order to maximise their potential to complete questionnaires (or other tools). It is often necessary for the practitioner or another person to assist the respondent through the completion of the questionnaire.

Practitioners also need to be alert to the 'right' timing and space for requesting involvement from respondents. This is especially relevant when dealing with persons who are in sensitive and stressful settings, such as intensive care units of hospitals. For example, it may be difficult to find an appropriate time to approach the parent of a child undergoing bone marrow transplant with a questionnaire; however, in some cases, they might be grateful for the distraction. In every situation, sensitivity to timing is key.

Self-administered questionnaires can be completed on paper and/or in an electronic format (see 'Conducting online surveys', page 106). While in some instances a paper copy may be perceived as friendlier and easier to complete, some respondents may prefer to work online. Paper questionnaires require considerable preparation time, including photocopying, distributing and ensuring that completed copies are returned. For the sake of efficiency, it is advisable to prioritise electronic distribution of questionnaires where possible. Different administration methods have different implications on the process of analysing the collected data (Phase 4); for example, narrative data collected in electronic form is already transcribed – something which can speed up the analysis process significantly.

When questionnaires cannot be self-administered, a facilitator can assist the respondent. In such cases, the choice of facilitator is essential. The practitioner may be a good choice of facilitator, since their thorough knowledge of the service and prior, trusting relationships with the respondents may elicit the fullest and richest responses; however, this very familiarity could equally be an obstacle. For example, respondents may withhold information that they consider to be criticism for fear of negatively affecting the care they are provided; equally, they may want to please the evaluator-practitioner by providing glowing accounts of the service. A less familiar facilitator (a staff member or a peer) may also have both advantages and disadvantages. As ever, thinking ahead and planning strategically avoids unexpected surprises.

## APPROACHING PEOPLE WITH LEARNING DISABILITIES

When people with learning disabilities are invited to complete a questionnaire (if and when appropriate), simple and structured questionnaires are essential.

- It is important to engage with the participant face to face, preferably with somebody familiar to the respondent who is skilled in communicating with them. Such a person – whether or not this is the practitioner – is more likely to be able to adapt or explain the questions to the individual. In addition, it may be useful to administer the questionnaire with the presence of a carer, parent or another person with whom they feel comfortable. Facilitators need to keep the right kind of 'distance' from the participant, so that they avoid leading or coercing their responses.

- Depending on the severity of the participant's learning disability, it may be necessary to alter the methods used in order to engage with them. It is important to engage on *their* terms and not try to make them fit a predetermined structure. Here, the practitioner needs to inform themselves about the methods of communication with which the participant is familiar (e.g. Picture Exchange Communication System, sign language or Makaton).

- It is important to create a relaxed and comfortable atmosphere, by keeping the right balance between formality and informality (Ball and Shanks, 2012). The participant should not feel judged or tested. This will help enable them to function to their highest potential and ultimately offer richer and more useful information.

- Simple and straightforward questions are always most effective. It is crucial to keep the number of questions to the minimum by focusing only on questions that directly address the evaluation aims.

- The person's attention span needs to be considered. In rare cases, the questionnaire may need to be broken down into sub-parts which are completed in intervals.

## APPROACHING PEOPLE WITH LIMITED SPEECH CAPACITY

Practitioners may want to involve the opinion of people who are cognitively able to express an opinion, yet whose speech capacity is limited (e.g. due to physical or brain disability). In this case, alternative non-verbal means of communication should be considered. The following suggestions may help:

- Consider participants' current form of communication. It may involve physical signals for 'yes' or 'no' such as blinking, squeezing a hand, eye movement or pointing, or may involve computerised communication systems.

- The questions should be altered in order to fit in with the range of words the participant is able to express. Asking 'yes' or 'no' questions may be most appropriate; alternatively, provide a list of options from which they can signal agreement or disagreement.

- Somebody who is used to communicating with the participant and understands the intricacies of their particular communication method must be present or should possibly be the person to administer the questionnaire. It is vital that a specialist be consulted in order to make best use of everybody's time and skill, and to ensure that the participant does not feel overwhelmed or frustrated.

## APPROACHING STAFF MEMBERS

Staff members are a very useful source of information since they often know service users on a professional as well as a personal level and will have interesting insights. However, it is important to assess the most efficient and effective ways to contact staff members. Some potential ways of ensuring that time with staff members is productive are outlined below:

- Leaving questionnaires in the staff room is not always the most effective way of getting staff members to participate in a questionnaire. It is more effective to approach people personally when inviting them to participate; this allows for a brief verbal explanation of the importance of the evaluation and answering any questions they may have.

- Consider staff timetables and choose a time sensitively so that it does not disrupt the flow of their daily routine. If the participant feels as if the questionnaire is getting in the way of their job, the answers will not be as full and detailed as they might have been otherwise.

- Consider organising a focus group questionnaire, where multiple staff members are talked through the questionnaire at once and their responses collected at the end.

- If the staff member is particularly busy, consider verbally administering the questionnaire while they carry out a simple task (e.g. while they are changing the sheets on a bed) – although this would not be ideal!

### Conducting online surveys

As implied earlier, online questionnaires can be cost-effective, as well as easier and faster to administer. Online questionnaires are preferred when a large number of participants is involved or when meeting participants is complicated. In these instances, sending the questionnaire electronically may be a better option. However, online questionnaires are more difficult to complete for those less confident in using computers or for those with limited access to the internet.

For online surveys, which generally target a large number of respondents, a thorough system for sending and collecting the survey questionnaires should be in place. This usually includes a mailing database where a tally of participants and their details can be kept: email addresses and all personal information must be stored safely.

## *Conducting interviews*

Interviews are time-consuming and carry additional personnel costs, yet they eliminate issues such as literacy level and visual impairment, and they provide an opportunity for clarifying the questions if needed. If not conducted by the evaluator, these clarifications (prompts and probes) should be outlined when briefing interviewers; this avoids bias and ensures standardisation of the questions asked. However, sensitive questions may be problematic in interviews because the respondent may feel obliged to respond in a way that is most socially acceptable.

Face-to-face interviews have many advantages: personal contact may increase the response rate; also, the use of visual aids is possible. Telephone interviews are less expensive in terms of travel expenses but provide limited control over the environment in which the interview is conducted, potentially compromising confidentiality. Question wording needs to be simple and it requires good hearing capacity from the respondent. If not facilitated by the evaluator, there is a risk that interviewers introduce bias by not asking the questions verbatim, modifying the questions or by inappropriate prompting. This risk can be reduced, but not fully eliminated by efficient briefing and training.

Evaluators need to bear in mind that interviews are usually conducted at a place and time that is convenient to the interviewee. However, interviews can take place at a distance, either via telephone or by using email, password-protected areas of websites or instant messaging (Jones, 2012; Jones and Dokter, 2012). Sometimes online interviews can 'free up' people and help them to be honest in their responses because they feel more 'anonymous'. Practitioners, however, need to be aware of potential safeguarding issues when using the internet. Chat rooms, newsrooms or groups, and email lists can present particular confidentiality risks.

When setting up interviews, it is important to ensure that the conditions are right. The following points should be considered when carrying out an interview:

- Make sure the interview space is quiet and private, and that enough time is available.

- Explain to the interviewee what kind of questions they will be asked and how long the interview will take (set a time limit), and agree with them how their answers will be used.

- Be prepared to hear both positive and negative feedback.

- Listen rather than lead.

- Do not speak too much or put words into the mouth of the interviewee.

- Think ahead about how to keep a record of what is said. For example:

  - Written notes under each question are the simplest record.

  - Taped interviews are time-consuming to transcribe, but they provide a complete record of the interview. A taped interview also offers the precise words people used, which can provide powerful evidence in reports. Interviewees should always be asked for permission before taping an interview (even where this has already been agreed in the participant information sheet) and assured that the recording will be safely stored and confidential. Be aware that recording can make people less likely to say what they really feel.

  - A combination of note-taking and recording can be useful. It is possible to make notes and when a particularly interesting comment is made, make a note of the time it occurs on the recorder. This will help to navigate back to that comment quickly when needed.

**The interviewer**

Self-awareness throughout: posture, gaze, voice, pace, tone.

Training in Self-observation (via video) helps refine interviewing technique

Important skills:
- *Active listening* (not talking too much, not putting words in mouth) – allowing & encouraging. Includes:
  - *Non-verbal listening* – facial expression, eye contact, head nods, gesture, physical proximity, posture
  - *Verbal listening* – responding to what has been said and moving it on. Being interviewee-centred.

Dangers:
- Interviewer anxiety
- Lack of confidence in technique
- Failure to appreciate active role of silence

```
┌─ ─ ─ ─ ─ ─ ─ ─ ─ ─ ┐
│   Guidelines for    │
│    Interviewing     │
└─ ─ ─ ─ ─ ─ ─ ─ ─ ─ ┘
```

**Interview management**

- **Introductory phase**
  - ❖ Setting – room & chairs OK?
  - ❖ Refreshments?
  - ❖ Dress – not careless
  - ❖ Recording equipment checked
  - ❖ Arrive on time
  - ❖ Handshake
  - ❖ Low-key manner

- **Opening development of the interview**
  - ❖ Explain purpose of interview and purpose of research
  - ❖ Explain why necessary to record & what you will be doing with recording
  - ❖ Turn on tape
  - ❖ Explain format of interview

- **Central core of the interview**
  - ❖ Observe schedule
  - ❖ Avoid establishing Q&A style interaction – go for responses, not answers
  - ❖ Make open questions GENUINELY open – avoid unnecessary prompting, suggestive tones of voice

- **Closing, both socially & content-wise**
  - ❖ Indicate that the end is coming – 'Now the last thing I want to ask you ...'
  - ❖ Summarise back to the interviewee so they can give you feedback
  - ❖ Turn off tape
  - ❖ Thank for participation and information
  - ❖ Tell them they will be able to see a summary of our findings next term.

**Prompts and probes**

*Prompts* are developed with the questions. They seek to help the interviewees to provide you with useful and relevant data. They are the aspects of each question we need all interviewees to address. They also offer a degree of standardisation between interviews – essential for subsequent analysis.

*Probes* are improvised supplementary questions or responses which you use to get interviewees to tell you more – to expand on their response, or part of it. They need to be simple, clear, direct, and SHORT. They may seek to fulfil the following functions:

- ❖ Clarification
- ❖ Showing appreciation and understanding
- ❖ Justification
- ❖ Relevance
- ❖ Giving an example
- ❖ Extending the narrative
- ❖ Accuracy
- ❖ Reflection

FIGURE 12 GUIDELINES FOR INTERVIEWING

It is not unusual to train colleagues or volunteers to conduct individual or group interviews for an evaluation. Another consideration is peer-to-peer interviewing, where project participants interview one another. This often elicits richer data than when the interviewer is seen as a figure of authority, or someone who is invested in the 'success' of the service or evaluation. In any of these situations, the interview workers need training, with several practice runs, role-playing and opportunities to troubleshoot and address difficulties that arise. In addition, debriefing after the interviews also helps to address concerns, encourage and generally give support. Figure 12 is an example of a leaflet prepared in order to support practitioners who were not used to conducting interviews.

## Conducting focus groups

The principles of conducting an effective interview can also be applied to conducting focus groups – a group interview. Focus groups can provide a forum for discussion where participants are motivated by each other's responses and are more likely to be reminded of personal experiences. The social situation can stimulate more discussion and therefore richer data. When running focus group discussions, evaluators should:

- Choose a range of people for a balance of views and attitudes.

- Remember that some people may be more open if their group leader or more senior staff are not there.

- Be aware of safeguarding issues with children, young people and vulnerable adults who cannot be left unsupervised by their carers. Permission is needed from designated persons in order to interview children, young people and vulnerable adults.

- Choose a quiet room, explain the agenda to the group, agree with them how their comments will be used and think about how to record what is said. As with individual interviews, taping the discussion provides a complete and accurate record, but it is time-consuming to transcribe.

- Leave time to summarise and agree the main points at the end.

If the focus group discussion is not recorded, it is worth considering having two people to run the group: one to facilitate the discussion and another to take notes – so that the facilitator does not have to write during the interview.

## Completing log-sheets

Although log-sheets are usually straightforward to use, they require a disciplined and systematic method of completion. In most cases, log-sheets gather information (such as attendance numbers or anecdotal feedback) that is difficult to remember retrospectively. Log-sheets need to be completed on an ongoing basis, immediately after a session or at the end of the working day.

Log-sheets are usually used over a period of weeks or months and can accumulate a large amount of information. For the sake of efficiency (especially with regard to data analysis, as explained in Phase 4) data can be entered directly into the electronic version of the log-sheet, usually designed on a spreadsheet.

## Completing reflective journals

Pre-designed and structured reflective journals ensure that these are used effectively and in a way that is useful to the evaluation, in contrast to participants being asked to keep their own notebooks. Evaluation participants generally keep their journals until the end of the project/evaluation period. Since participants often forget to complete or return journals at the end of a project, they need regular reminding. It may be necessary to schedule time at the end of every session for people to write in their journals. Also, where there is likelihood of people losing their journals, it may be prudent for these to be handed out and collected each time.

## Conducting observations

Observations are generally recorded systematically by writing notes, ticking checklists or by dictating observation notes into pocket audio recorders. Evaluators may record observations on the spot (e.g. while an arts activity is happening); at other times, they may record their observations after they have left the situation (e.g. at the end of a session). In each case, it is important to record the date, location and any other characteristic aspects of the observation; this will help to correspond each set of observation data with other data collected on the same day or location.

### Collecting secondary data and supplementary material

As explained earlier (Sections 1.3 and 1.4, pages 59–62), an evaluation project often uses pre-existing information which has been collected previously for another purpose (i.e. secondary data), as well as supplementary material (i.e. supportive and complementary material which illustrates the evaluation data).

Even if secondary data is pre-existing (and does not need to be collected or generated for the evaluation), evaluators still need to be systematic and proactive in identifying it and selecting relevant material. Information that belongs to an organisation (e.g. attendance numbers or demographic profiles) may need permission to be used for evaluative purposes. A system developed for selecting and storing secondary data for the purposes of the evaluation will also be necessary.

As for generating supplementary material, which usually involves taking photographs, audio and video recordings, all necessary equipment needs to be tested beforehand to ensure optimal quality of photographs, soundtracks and films. Importantly, relevant consent forms need to be ready for signing before any recording begins and before using images in any public capacity (for further information on consenting procedures, see 'A Note on Ethics', page 161).

## 3.2 The 'right' time and the 'right' participants

It is generally considered good practice to collect evaluation data at different points during a project. Choosing the 'right' time depends on the evaluation aims and the set-up of a service or project. In some cases (e.g. ongoing services), collecting pre-project evaluation data is not possible. Where a service has a finite duration, collecting data before, during and after its completion helps to document change through reference to an established base line (i.e. information about service users' skills or wellbeing before taking part in the service).

Since there is no formula for when it is best to evaluate a service, practitioners need to make informed decisions about the different times and durations of the data collection phase. Thorough and detailed planning (Phase 1) helps to avoid last-minute decisions and last-minute data collection.

In addition to identifying the 'right' time, the 'right' participants need to be identified. As in any evidence-gathering project, evaluation requires some kind of sampling – that is, targeting or selecting participants (and material) to be assessed. An evaluation project cannot assess all procedures and/or people involved in a service; for example, those who were directly involved in the service could be targeted specifically. While administering the collection tools, evaluators need to be alert to the sampling criteria that have been established during the planning of the evaluation (Phase 1).

## 3.3 An evaluation community and shared ownership

The evaluator's attitude is crucial during the collection phase of the evaluation. Effective evaluation is not a solo activity but involves a community of people. Creating a sense of shared ownership and responsibility for an evaluation project ensures a smooth collection process of data and supplementary material. The following tips can help all involved to experience a sense of shared ownership:

- Communicate explicitly the aims of the evaluation and why people's participation is important.

- Help participants to remember important dates, such as the deadline for submitting their completed questionnaires. Different reminders can be sent at different times.

- Be available, listen and answer people's questions, ideas or concerns.

- Be honest about the aim of the evaluation, the role of the participants and the things not known.

- Encourage people to find meaning and feel that they want to be part of the evaluation; otherwise, participating will be a burden for them.

- Explain to participants the collection process and let them know if there are any ways through which they can help (e.g. reminding of other participants to complete their questionnaire).

- Make the evaluation process visible in the organisation. This can involve increased contact with the participants and notices (such as posters) in different areas of the organisation, including staff rooms and waiting or other public areas.

Imagination and creativity do not only belong within arts-based practices. Participants need to be engaged with – and excited about – the evaluation, and this requires an enthusiastic evaluator-practitioner. The sense of an evaluation community can be enhanced further by introducing creative and imaginative methods of administering and collecting data and material. Arts therapists' and arts & health practitioners' skill to be creative and think 'out of the box' is particularly relevant here, as they can think beyond the usual or traditional ways of collecting material. Of course, imaginative collection methods require creative analysis methods (Phase 4). Therefore, practitioners need to think from the beginning about how they will analyse collected data and material.

The use of a 'postbox' helps to collect completed questionnaires in a creative and playful way. A postbox is also a visual reference and reminder – especially in organisations where most people work part-time, and colleagues and peers are administering the evaluation tools (e.g. questionnaires) on days when the practitioner is absent. Postboxes need to be located in central points of a building, be clearly labelled and have attached a pocket with extra blank questionnaires.

The use of a postbox is also useful where spontaneous, unstructured comments and feedback are invited. A set of blank postcards beside a box, with a request for people to jot down their comments during or after an activity and 'post' the postcard in the box, is a useful way of collecting spontaneous comments. These kinds of responses usually indicate particular issues which need to be discussed in more detail and addressed.

Likewise, a comments book at an exhibition, a choir rehearsal or in the waiting area of a clinic can allow people to document their experiences freely, and therefore give practitioners a sense of how the service is experienced.

Boards or 'graffiti' walls are a more public version of a comments book. To help structure these kinds of comments, practitioners can invite responses on a particular aspect of the service. This informal technique often engages younger people and can be particularly useful at conferences, where people can add comments as they pass by.

The integration of such creative ways of collecting data and material often makes the provision of feedback exciting for participants and helps the evaluation process to become part of people's overall service experience.

Once the collection of data and supplementary material is completed (Phase 3), it is not enough to simply gather and present the raw data in a report; it needs to be processed and analysed (Phase 4).

# Phase 4

## Processing Data and Supplementary Material

Data comes in various forms – numeric, narrative, pictorial and auditory. Phase 4 takes these different types of data at face value, and considers how to prepare, collate and process them in order to contribute to the evaluation findings.

## 4.1 Preparing and collating data for analysis and keeping track

Before any analysis, the 'raw' unprocessed data and material need to be prepared. This generally involves ensuring that everything is clearly labelled and organised into particular formats (e.g. transcriptions and data spreadsheets) for the purposes of analysis.

Organising the raw data can be a lengthy procedure and data is usually organised some considerable time after the data collection originally began. For example, in a year-long evaluation, the process of data analysis may not start for a year after the first set of data was collected. Because of this, it is essential to be able to keep track of raw material by having a separate document which explains the labelling and storing system.

Each data item needs to be identified clearly after data collection. Methods of identification can include:

- numbering each completed questionnaire with a unique number and date of completion

- use of colour codes for different types or forms of data, or different periods of data collection

- clearly labelled dates of interviews or focus groups on transcription sheet headers, with pages numbers
- numbering of each line of interview/focus group transcripts
- different colour-coded box files for storing data collected at different times or locations.

To keep track of each of these coded methods, a separate spreadsheet with explanations of all dates, identifying labels and storing systems is an essential part of organisation, preparation and the ethical obligations surrounding data. Systematic and safe data storage is critical and ensures that any evaluation material collected is not mislaid. Evaluation material can contain personal information about people and therefore needs to be (i) kept private and confidential in a secure place and (ii) easily accessible by the practitioner-evaluator.

Most evaluators develop their own systems for preparing data, and since this largely depends on the analysis method, the guidelines provided here will need to be tailored according to each evaluation. For example, detailed notes from an observation or focus group need to be typed up and organised according to the section headings of the observation or questions asked in the focus group; audio recordings of interviews or focus groups need to be transcribed; while data from questionnaires completed by hand should be entered into an electronic spreadsheet and compiled question by question.

Collating data from questionnaires involves forward planning, preferably at the stage when the questionnaire is being prepared. Some simple guidelines are presented here.

Data from all completed questionnaires are normally entered into a single spreadsheet that corresponds to each question in the questionnaire. The figures below provide an example of the entering of questionnaire responses into a spreadsheet. Each completed questionnaire is labelled with the participant number when it is returned – for example, P1, P2, P3, etc. This labelling helps to keep track of the data origin, and ensures that responses from a questionnaire are not entered twice by accident. Figure 13 shows Participant 4's response to question 5 of a questionnaire.

Figure 14 collates all of the participants' responses to question 5 in a spreadsheet.

**5a. How would you describe your experience in music therapy in Hodderson House?** *(Please tick as many as apply)*

- ☐ It is boring
- ☑ It helps me to express what I am feeling
- ☐ It makes me feel frustrated
- ☑ I enjoy playing the instruments
- ☐ It makes me feel anxious
- ☑ I like playing music with other people
- ☐ It is too noisy
- ☑ It helps me to feel more positive about myself

- ☐ It helps me to relax
- ☐ It makes me feel isolated
- ☐ Not sure

(P4)

**5b. Any further comments?:** *(optional)*

*It makes it easier to connect with people.*

FIGURE 13 EXAMPLE OF A PARTICIPANT'S RESPONSES

| A | B | C | D | E | F | G | H | I | J |
|---|---|---|---|---|---|---|---|---|---|
| 42 **5a. How would you describe your experience in music therapy sessions at Hodderson House?** | | | | | | | | | |
| 43 | P1 | P2 | P3 | P4 | P5 | P6 | P7 | P8 | Total |
| 44 It is boring | | | | | | | | | 0 |
| 45 It helps me to express what I am feeling | 1 | | | 1 | 1 | 1 | 1 | | 5 |
| 46 It makes me feel frustrated | | 1 | | | | 1 | | | 2 |
| 47 I enjoy playing the instruments | | 1 | | 1 | 1 | 1 | | | 4 |
| 48 It makes me feel anxious | | | | | | | | | 0 |
| 49 I like playing music with other people | | 1 | 1 | 1 | 1 | 1 | 1 | | 6 |
| 50 It is too noisy | 1 | 1 | | | | 1 | | | 3 |
| 51 It helps me to feel more positive about myself | | 1 | 1 | 1 | 1 | 1 | 1 | | 6 |
| 52 It helps me to relax | 1 | 1 | 1 | | 1 | 1 | 1 | 1 | 7 |
| 53 It makes me feel isolated | | | | | | | | | 0 |
| 54 Not sure | | | | | | | | | 0 |
| 55 | | | | | | | | | |
| 56 **5b. Comments** | | | | | | | | | |
| 57 P3 - A welcome change from a day of sitting alone. | | | | | | | | | |
| 58 P4 - It makes it easier to connect with people | | | | | | | | | |
| 59 P6 - It makes me feel that I am capable of playing music. | | | | | | | | | |
| 60 | | | | | | | | | |

FIGURE 14 EXAMPLE OF A SPREADSHEET OF COLLATED RESPONSES

Electronically collected data can automatically be converted into a spreadsheet of collated responses. However, in some cases, each response is automatically converted into a spreadsheet of its own; in these instances, all data should be compiled together as described above. Once data is collated and prepared into in a manageable format, it is ready for processing and analysis.

## 4.2 Processing data in narrative forms

Data in narrative forms is usually processed as qualitative data (although in some cases it may be quantifiable). Thematic analysis is a common analysis method for such types of data. Although this method can be informed by different methodological frameworks such as phenomenology or grounded theory (Smith and Osborn, 2003; Starks and Trinidad, 2007), this guide focuses on the practical steps that can help practitioners to break down the analytic process.

The underlying concept of thematic analysis is the identification of emerging themes through clustering small segments into larger meaning units. The different levels of meaning units are usually named as 'codes', 'categories' and 'themes'. These meaning units need to emerge naturally from the data and should not be forced to fit into prescribed 'boxes'. The basic system of thematic analysis is to go through stages of coding and categorising until a manageable number of themes is evident. Depending on the amount and complexity of the collected data and material, thematic analysis may consist of two, three or more stages of coding and categorising.

The analytic steps described below can be applied to any type of data and material that is in narrative form, including interview or focus group transcripts, observation notes or answers to open-ended questions from a questionnaire.

### i. Coding

Coding is a 'technical term for analytic labeling' (Ansdell and Pavlicevic, 2001, p.150), where the aim is to organise the data. Coding requires reading the raw data and identifying the natural segments within the ideas expressed in the text (this may be only a sentence long). It is important to be sure that these codes are identified in light of their relevance to the evaluation aims. Part of the coding process may involve discarding data that has no relevance to the evaluation aims. Each segment is then labelled with a code (a word or short phrase) that represents the ideas in the segment.

Qualitative data that is already in a predetermined structure, such as collated responses to an open-ended survey question, already segmented into different ideas, can be coded without additional segmenting.

## ii. Categorising

These codes can then be grouped into larger meaning units forming categories. By categorising the codes, similar or related codes are grouped so that distinctions can be made between the various ideas in the data. Categorising is the stage between coding and the eventual identification of themes in the data. The categorising process may need to take place multiple times if the data is particularly dense. Indeed, Edwards and Talbot (1999) describe the process of establishing categories as progressive and provide advice for evaluators going through the process:

1. Develop possible categories.

2. Code your label data according to them (as many data as possible).

3. Test the accuracy of the categories (do the codes fit into the categories, or is there overspill?).

4. Firm up category boundaries by identifying overlaps.

5. Discard weak categories (those which only contain one or two codes).

6. Create new categories if necessary.

Ultimately, categorisation should allow practitioners to progress to the next stage: identifying themes.

### *iii. Identifying themes*

By further grouping the categories, themes emerge from the data. These themes should then be described in the evaluation findings with reference to and quotation of the original data that makes up the theme; select representative quotes from the raw data. Themes may contain conflicting ideas about similar topics; this sort of occurrence will be discussed in your descriptions of the emergent themes. There is no set number of themes that is 'best'; the number of emergent themes reflects the richness of the data analysed.

Although this thematic analysis process is for analysis of an interview transcript or a group of answers to a question, practitioners may find that within the same evaluation, similar themes develop from different data sources. Practitioners can then group these themes together and deal with them under the same section of the evaluation findings.

Figure 15 provides an example of thematic analysis, while Figure 16 is a simplified, schematic representation of the analytic steps described above. In cases where a large number of narratives have been collected, it is worth exploring the possibilities of using specialised computer software for qualitative analysis (e.g. NVivo and ATLAS.ti). Practitioners need to consider, however, that the use of such software often requires learning how to use it effectively, and at times software can be expensive.

| Transcripts (staff questionnaire responses) | Codes | Categories | Themes |
|---|---|---|---|
| **Physiotherapist:**<br>1 Tuesdays have a better atmosphere,<br>2 and it's nice to see and hear patients<br>3 participating in a 'normal' activity,<br>4 when they spend so much time<br>5 sitting or lying, doing nothing. Raised<br>6 morale. Encouraged me to take up<br>7 the piano again!! | Improved workplace environment<br><br>A sense of normality<br><br>Raised morale<br>Staff's personal engagement with music | Music therapy enhances workplace environment and relationships<br><br>Music therapy helps with job-related tasks | Music therapy impacts on the organisation<br><br>Music therapy impacts on staff |
| **Occupational therapist:**<br>8 It has helped me to gain more ideas<br>9 for rehabilitation and helped me gain<br>10 a better working relationship with<br>11 the more withdrawn patients. It has<br>12 also impacted on my personal mood<br>13 and makes work a nicer place. | Advancement of working ideas<br><br>Improved staff-patient relationships<br>Staff's mood<br>Improved workplace environment | Music therapy increases staff's motivation to do music | |

FIGURE 15 EXAMPLE OF THEMATIC ANALYSIS

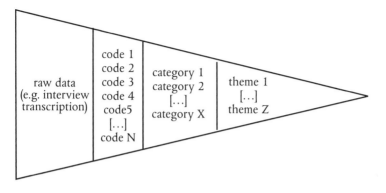

FIGURE 16 THEMATIC ANALYSIS PROCESS

## *Writing case vignettes*

As discussed previously, secondary data is often collected in order to write case studies or vignettes. Case studies are generally used to present material from everyday practice; within the context of an evaluation, descriptive accounts of real-life cases are an effective way of illustrating and contextualising the themes that have emerged from the rest of the data. Case studies and vignettes provide a context for the data and help the reader to engage with the experience of the service users who access the practice.

The term 'case study' covers a wide range of designs (such as single case studies, series of case studies and narrative case studies), each of which can be used for different research (and evaluation) purposes (Aldridge, D., 2005a; Aldridge, G., 2005).

> Case study designs are research strategies based upon empirical investigation. A particular case is identified and located in content, which may be social, temporal or spatial. It is the bounding of the case in a context that makes the case study a 'case' study – the case may be a person, several persons, a group or a situation. (Aldridge, 2005b, pp.10–11)

From this point of view, a case study can concern a service user, a practitioner, a group, a course of therapy or a therapeutic method, depending on what the practitioner wants to illustrate. It is important to remember that the power of case studies lies in the fact that they are context-specific.

Also, the flexible designs and formats of case studies (Robson, 2002) can vary significantly in the depth of their exploration. Case vignettes, for example, are usually briefer than other case formats and are particularly helpful for complementing fact and figures with real-life examples. They can be used to illustrate evaluation findings with specific examples which provide 'inside' moments of practice; they also help to engage evaluation audiences who value personal stories and evidence of experience over statistics and figures.

When writing case vignettes, it is important to consider the service aims and the evaluation aims; this may help determine which accounts are most relevant to the evaluation. The structure and content of a vignette should have a specific focus, since it is by nature a brief form of writing. Each vignette tells a story with a beginning, middle and end. Figure 17 is designed to help ensure that practitioners consider all basic features of a case vignette; however, not all features will be necessary in all cases. Although Figure 17 focuses on case vignettes written with a service user in focus, similar principles apply in case vignettes with other focuses (e.g. a group of service users or a staff member).

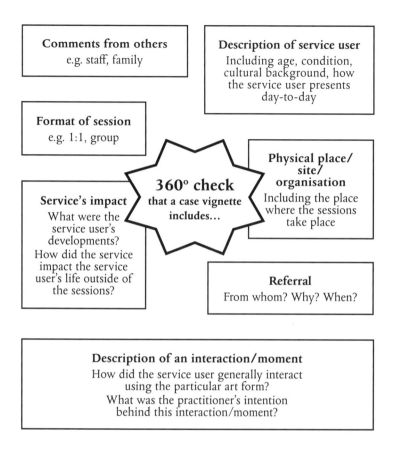

FIGURE 17 ASPECTS TO BE CONSIDERED IN CASE VIGNETTES

In addition to those outlined in Figure 17, when writing a vignette for evaluation purposes it is worth considering the following points:

- Provide a title for each vignette that relates to the themes identified in the evaluation findings (e.g. communication and social skills, mobility, emotional expression).

- Write in the first person: 'I matched on the piano the intensity of Bryan's drum playing...'

- Use direct quotes from service users, staff and/or family.

- Use photos of the depicted person(s) in action – if permission is refused, practitioners can use another relevant photo (e.g. a photo of an instrument mentioned in the vignette).

- If writing several vignettes, provide a range of work (e.g. individual, group work, choir, spontaneous interaction, family work), describe work in different scales (e.g. from a moment to a therapy course), and describe low or difficult issues (not only 'magic' moments) – this helps people to understand the complexity of the work.

- Keep vignettes brief, simple and accessible.

- Ensure that each vignette tells a story with a beginning (introduction), middle and end, or that it describes a service user or group before, during and after engagement with the service.

These guidelines act as a starting point and practitioners are invited to elaborate or edit as necessary. Although service users are generally the focus of a case vignette, families, staff and visitors may also be the focus, if this in line with the evaluation aims. Case vignettes are often very similar to stories written for internal reports or communication/publicity reports; however, the focus of such reports is very different to a vignette written for evaluative purposes. They serve different aims and are often addressed to different audiences. Figure 18 gives an example of a vignette written for evaluative purposes.

What is the
location?

Who referred
the service user
to music therapy
and why they
were referred

Where did the
sessions take
place?

Service user's
response

Description
of service
user (age,
diagnosis)

Description
of service
user (how
they present
day-to-day)

Music
therapist's
intentions

Music
therapist's
technique

How did
they interact
in music?

Impact on
outside life

T is aged 6 and was recently diagnosed with cancer. He arrived on the ward from the Intensive Care Unit with a tracheotomy and so was unable to speak above a whisper. The ward teacher referred him for music therapy as he was finding it hard to concentrate, being edgy and twitchy. His parents reported that this was very different from his pre-hospital behaviour which was focused and hardworking.

As I was preparing to go and see T, I was hoping that music therapy would give him an opportunity to have a 'voice' through the use of musical instruments and be able to regain some sense of control which was largely lost due to his condition.

I went to see him while he was in bed, bringing my trolley full of instruments and at first sharing a keyboard with him as he lay in bed. He quickly became involved in playing and musically taking the lead and he showed enjoyment when I mirrored or musically 'commented' on what he played. At first he played random notes, enjoying making lots of noisy sounds. As the session progressed he seemed to think more carefully about which notes to play, creating careful musical lines and we were able to 'converse' with question-and-answer phrases.

Following this first session T has eagerly come to music therapy sessions each time he is in hospital. He is now able to speak and even after just being hooked up to his chemo he will get himself up and hurry down to the music room.

The music therapy sessions allowed him to focus and have a positive experience during his stay on the ward. He was not just able to be expressive himself but also enjoyed involving his parents in shared music making. He was able to take the lead and be the one in control of shaping the music and the part his parents and I took in it.

> Developments in music therapy

'I like to play loudly and I don't like it when the sessions finish.'

T (age 6)

'We thought the music sessions he had with you were great especially the first one as this was when he had just had the tracheostomy and wasn't speaking and was unable to get out of bed, he really enjoyed it and we could see the normal happy T again for a short while.'

T's father

FIGURE 18 EXAMPLE OF A CASE VIGNETTE

## 4.3 Processing data in numeric forms

In basic terms, quantitative analysis is simply a way of processing data in numeric forms. It can range from calculating simple facts through to more complex calculations and statistical tests. Although quantitative analysis can be a powerful tool for evaluation, it rarely represents a complete picture of any practice without qualitative analysis of data in narrative forms to complement it.

There are two strands to quantitative data analysis. These strands are known as *descriptive statistics* and *inferential statistics*.

### Descriptive statistics

Descriptive statistics help to organise and describe features of a set of numeric data. The aim of descriptive statistics is to organise and describe data so that it is easier to understand. That is, the results of descriptive statistical analysis cannot be generalised to a larger group (i.e. inferences about a larger group cannot be made on the basis of descriptive statistics). Descriptive statistical measures are known as measures of 'central tendency' and measures of 'variability'. Measures of central tendency include the mean, range, median and mode, while measures of variability include the standard deviation.

## MEAN, RANGE, MEDIAN AND MODE

The mean, range, median and mode are four kinds of 'averages' that can be used to organise data. There are many types of average in statistics, but these are the four most common and most likely to be useful in the context of analysing data for evaluative purposes. Providing the average of a data set is simply a description of what is already there; it is not an interpretation of the data but a way to describe the data that may make it easier for the reader to engage with.

- The *mean* is the most common measure: it is the sum of all the values (e.g. total number of service users) divided by the count (e.g. number of weeks). This type of calculation is useful for calculating, for example, the average number of service users an arts service reaches in one week.

- The *range* is the difference between the lowest and highest values.

- The *median* is the middle number in a sorted list of values. To find the median, values have to be listed in numerical order, so the original list may have to be reordered first. There might not be a middle number if there is an even quantity of data entries; in this case, the mean value of the two middle numbers should be taken.

- The *mode* is the number that occurs most often in a set of numbers. If a data set has two modes, this is described as a 'bimodal' distribution. Having more than two modes is called 'multimodal'. If no number is repeated, then there is no mode for the data.

Table 5 shows how the aforementioned measures are calculated, illustrated by a fictional example in which a practitioner wants to show how many service users have accessed a service over a period of five weeks. In this context, it would be useful to know on average how many service users have access to the service per week, and also how constant or variable attendance to the service is.

**TABLE 5 Example of mean, range, median and mode**

| Number of weeks | Week 1 | Week 2 | Week 3 | Week 4 | Week 5 | Total number of service users |
|---|---|---|---|---|---|---|
| Number of service users | 6 | 10 | 10 | 12 | 14 | 52 |

**Mean** = 10.4 clients per week (i.e. 52 clients / 5 weeks)
**Range** = 8 (i.e. 14–6)
**Median** = 10 (i.e. 6, 10, **10**, 12, 14)
**Mode** = 10 (i.e. 6, **10**, **10**, 12, 14)

## STANDARD DEVIATION (SD)

The standard deviation is the average distance that a set of numbers vary from the mean number of that set of numbers. In other words, it is a measure of how spread-out numbers are. It is a measure of the variability of the set of numbers. It is usually referred to as SD or with the symbol σ (the Greek letter sigma). This measure allows us to have a sense of how much the numbers vary – a small standard deviation indicates that the set of numbers is fairly constant, whereas a large standard deviation would indicate that the numbers fluctuate a lot. To find the standard deviation, one needs to find the square root of the variance (which is the average of the squared differences from the mean). The formula is:

$SD = \sqrt{\text{Variance}}$

**Variance** = [(No. of clients in week 1 – mean)$^2$ + ... + (No. of clients in week 6 – mean)$^2$] / Total number of weeks

An example is provided below, drawing from the numbers given in Table 5.

**Variance** = $[(6 - 10.4)^2 + (10 - 10.4)^2 + (10 - 10.4)^2 + (12 - 10.4)^2 + (14 - 10.4)^2] / 5 = 7.04$

**SD** = $\sqrt{}$ Variance = $\sqrt{}$ 7.04

**SD** = 2.6533

As shown in Figure 19, we can now identify which numbers of clients are within the SD (2.6533). Within the context of this example, it helps us see how consistent attendance to the service is week-to-week. Here, we can see that weeks 2, 3 and 4 all fall within the standard rate of attendance; however, week 1 is below the standard rate of attendance and week 5 is above the standard rate of attendance. Since these two weeks fall outside the remit of what is statistically 'normal' for this set of data, it may be worth commenting on why this might be. For this fictional example, at week 1, many service users were attending an alternative meeting that was scheduled on the same day; while at week 5, some new service users accessed the service.

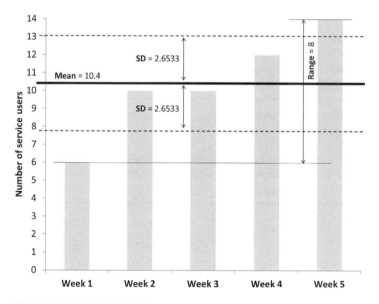

FIGURE 19 SD, MEAN AND RANGE

## *Visual representation*

Numeric findings can be organised using a range of visual representations, such as bar charts and pie charts. The advantage of a diagram is that it can provide the reader with a quick overview of the findings without long written explanations. However, using the right type of diagram for the right type of finding is key to ensuring that readers can understand the findings quickly and easily. Practitioners may have to experiment with different types of diagrams until they find the one they think is the most appropriate in each case. Experimenting with different diagrammatic possibilities is simple once data has been inserted into a spreadsheet. Certain findings may be represented better using percentages or absolute values or mean numbers. However, there are no rules of thumb here; it is simply a case of deciding on the clearest representation of the data in each single case. People's ratings of different aspects of a music therapy service, for instance, can be represented using mean numbers (Table 6).

**TABLE 6 Mean staff ratings of aspects of music therapy work**

| Aspects of music therapy work | Mean ratings 1 ('poor') to 5 ('excellent') |
|---|---|
| Clients' attendance of music therapy sessions | 4.3 |
| Quality of communication between music therapist and staff | 4.1 |
| Parents'/carers' attendance of music therapy sessions | 3.7 |

It is often useful to show rates of attendance in a graph, rather than simply stating the mean attendance. This allows the reader to see the attendance ratings growing or shrinking in relation to time (see Figure 20). Once the raw data is collated into a spreadsheet, these graphs can be made using Microsoft Office Excel or similar programs.

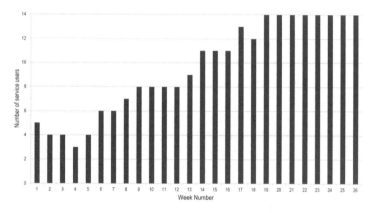

FIGURE 20 WEEKLY ATTENDANCE TO A GROUP MUSIC THERAPY SESSION OVER A PERIOD OF 26 WEEKS

## Analysis of the Likert scale

The traditional method for analysing a Likert scale is to code the responses by assigning a numerical value to each rating. Suppose, for example, respondents are asked how much they agree or disagree with a statement. Their responses might be coded as follows: strongly disagree = 1, disagree = 2, neutral = 3, agree = 4, strongly agree = 5. Then practitioners can depict the range of responses using bar charts that display the number and percentage of respondents who expressed agreement, impartiality or disagreement with each statement in the questionnaire.

Practitioners may also use descriptive statistics to organise the data. However, in the case of the Likert scale, it is not appropriate to calculate the mean value of the responses because this data is ordinal in nature. Alternatively, it is possible to organise the Likert scale data with the mode (i.e. the most frequent response). For example, if 'agree' was the most frequent response to a statement, 'agree' would be the mode response to that statement.

### Analysis of the semantic differential

An average response (ranking) needs to be calculated for each statement and can be plotted on the graph. In some cases, a visual representation of pre- and post- responses may be appropriate. Figure 21 is an example of the results of the semantic differential comparing the mean (average) of parents' responses at the beginning (continuous line) and end (dotted line) of their children's course of music therapy. The differences for each statement can be statistically analysed.

It is not uncommon for respondents to circle the space between numbers (instead of a number). In such cases, practitioners can score the dimension using a midpoint. For example, if a participant circles the space between point 1 and point 2, the practitioner can assign the score as 1.5. Results can be presented in a figure or practitioners can list the average scores for each statement.

### Analysis of ranking

Practitioners can use descriptive statistics to organise the data yielded from ranked responses. Finding the mean response can be particularly illustrative in these cases. Drawing from the data example given in Section 2.2, a simple representation of the fictitious responses is given in Table 7.

**Drawing from your experience of bringing your child to music therapy, please rate each of the following...** *(Please circle one number for each statement)*

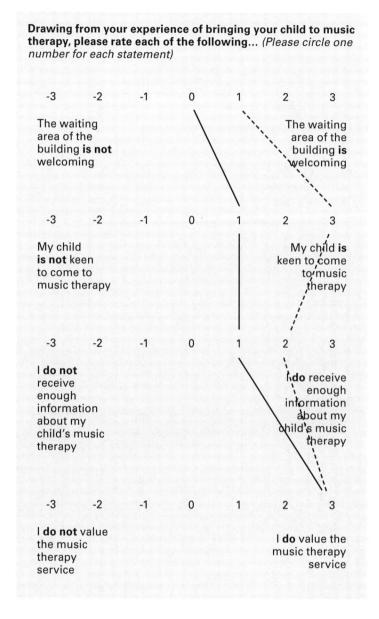

| -3 | -2 | -1 | 0 | 1 | 2 | 3 |

The waiting area of the building **is not** welcoming

The waiting area of the building **is** welcoming

| -3 | -2 | -1 | 0 | 1 | 2 | 3 |

My child **is not** keen to come to music therapy

My child **is** keen to come to music therapy

| -3 | -2 | -1 | 0 | 1 | 2 | 3 |

I **do not** receive enough information about my child's music therapy

I **do** receive enough information about my child's music therapy

| -3 | -2 | -1 | 0 | 1 | 2 | 3 |

I **do not** value the music therapy service

I **do** value the music therapy service

FIGURE 21 EXAMPLE OF ANALYSIS OF SEMANTIC DIFFERENTIAL SCALE

**TABLE 7 Sum of ranked responses**

| Interest | Participant 1 | Participant 2 | Participant 3 | Participant 4 | Sum per statement |
|---|---|---|---|---|---|
| singing | 1 | 5 | 5 | 5 | 16 |
| listening to music | 3 | 6 | 4 | 6 | 19 |
| going to concerts | 2 | 7 | 3 | 7 | 19 |
| playing music with other people | 6 | 1 | 6 | 8 | 21 |
| playing in a band | 5 | 8 | 2 | 3 | 18 |
| moving to music | 4 | 4 | 7 | 1 | 16 |
| drumming | 7 | 3 | 8 | 4 | 22 |
| talking about music | 8 | 2 | 1 | 2 | 13 |

Please rank your interests in the following (please write a number in each box, from 1 = very interested, to 8 = not at all interested)

Next, the statements can be ordered from highest (or most positive) score to lowest (or least positive) score according to the sum of each statement; however, the average responses give a clearer picture of the findings. To find the average for each statement ('singing', 'listening to music', 'drumming', etc.), calculate the total sum of the responses to the statement divided by the total number of responses – that is, the total sum of responses per statement, divided by the total number of participant responses. In Table 8 below, it is the lowest average that signals participants' greatest interest, while the highest average signals the least interest (i.e. participants are most interested in 'talking about music', yet are the least interested in 'drumming').

**TABLE 8 Averages of ranked responses**

| Interest | Total | Average |
|---|---|---|
| talking about music | 13 | 3.25 |
| singing | 16 | 4 |
| moving to music | 16 | 4 |
| playing in a band | 18 | 4.5 |
| listening to music | 19 | 4.75 |
| going to concerts | 19 | 4.75 |
| playing music with other people | 21 | 5.25 |
| drumming | 22 | 5.5 |

## Inferential statistics

In contrast to descriptive statistics, inferential statistics provide ways of testing the reliability of the findings of a study and inferring characteristics from a small group of participants for larger groups of people – it is a way of inferring generalisability and is relevant when a study takes a small population as representative of a larger one. Inferential statistics traditionally make use of a hypothesis – the data is examined in order to prove or falsify the hypothesis. Inferential statistics are therefore not immediately relevant for evaluations, which do not involve the stating of a hypothesis or wishing to generalise beyond the particular population or service questioned. Inferential statistics are more relevant in research contexts.

Common examples of inferential statistics are the t-test, analysis of variance (ANOVA) and chi-square tests which can be used to calculate the probability of the findings being representative of the population that the sample represents. Other examples include linear regression analyses, logistic regression analyses, correlation analyses, structural equation modelling, and survival analyses.

## 4.4 Processing supplementary material

Many arts-based practitioners collect material such as photographs, films, sound recordings, poems and artwork. This kind of material can be significantly time-consuming to prepare and edit; for example, photographing artwork, editing photographs, selecting soundtracks and burning them on to CD, selecting film material, designing and creating CD and DVD labels and covers. The selection and processing of such material needs to be informed by the rest of the data gathered to ensure that this complements and enhances the evaluation findings.

Phase 4 has introduced some basic ideas and concepts with regard to various ways of processing data and supplementary material for evaluative purposes. For in-depth explanation of particular data analysis methods, however, practitioners may need to consult specialised handbooks and web resources. Once all data and material have been processed, practitioners are ready to start drafting the evaluation outputs.

# Phase 5

## Drafting Outputs

Once evaluation data and material have been processed, the findings are ready to be assembled and disseminated through a number of outputs and formats. While the most common method of disseminating evaluation findings is the evaluation report, which is the primary focus of Phases 5 and 6, posters and flyers, website blogs, live presentations to stakeholders or conference presentations offer multiple avenues for reporting. These should ideally form part of any dissemination strategy from the start of an evaluation; the amount of work and resources that go into any evaluation warrant multiple kinds of outputs and dissemination pathways.

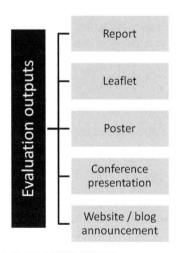

FIGURE 22 EXAMPLES OF EVALUATION OUTPUTS

## 5.1 Planning the drafting

Drafting evaluation outputs is an undervalued and underestimated aspect of the evaluation process. It is not uncommon to feel that once data and material have been processed, the hard work and time-consuming phase is over. However, communicating findings and writing up evaluation reports is the most important part of the process. Without communicating clearly and accurately, evaluation commissioners and service stakeholders will remain unconvinced by findings, however robust these might be. Not only does it take time to write succinct and communicative prose, create charts and diagrams, or create verbal and/or slide-show presentations, additional time is needed for multiple readers to check drafts and make suggestions; this is why drafting outputs forms a distinct phase that is prior to finalising and disseminating.

### *Communicating an evaluation*

Findings need to be communicated effectively. While good organisation, complete information and clear writing are key to the success of any document design, less obvious techniques make outputs engaging, accessible and effective.

Knowing the audience is fundamental:

- How are they likely to interpret the information?

- What other kinds of records do they generally keep, what documents do they generally use, and to what purposes?

- How will the evaluation output (and the choice of format) add to, extend or challenge their interests and engagements with the project?

Producing effective documentation (such as the aesthetic design) is about being clear about who the *primary* audience is. Since it is impossible to satisfy every reader in a single document, strategic planning is needed. While often it is necessary to target the report towards the evaluation commissioners, more often it is in everybody's interests for the findings to be available to as many audiences as possible. So while it is wise to bear in mind the primary target readers, if a range of audiences need to be addressed in a single document, the evaluation report needs to be planned so that each audience can identify and navigate towards the section that applies to them, and safely skim through the sections that do not concern them. The most effective strategy is undoubtedly to produce multiple outputs for the same evaluation findings (e.g. a written report, poster presentation and conference presentation).

### Reporting formats

Written evaluation reports have traditionally been considered a long and rather dull read. A clear advantage of a substantial written evaluation report is that it provides a comprehensive and explicit record of the impact or workings of a service. This can become a reference archive when starting future arts-based services. Written reports are the ubiquitous way of communicating systematic evaluations with funders and managers.

While useful, and generally the most comprehensive of all formats, it would be disingenuous to consider them the only necessary output. This is especially so when reporting on arts-based practices, for which complementary and creative ways of reporting may be far more appropriate and capture more closely the service's character.

The choice of the type of reporting format needs to be an informed decision. For a start, it needs to be meaningful to the audience – or audiences. It may well be that more than one format is needed; by considering multiple ways to present findings, different audiences can be reached for different purposes, in different situations. Also, a range of reporting formats can be used in similar situations at the same time for optimal impact. For example, illustrated presentations to colleagues, participants and advocacy groups; posters and presentations at strategically selected conferences; writing in newsletters, publishing a journal article or writing an evaluation summary for relevant websites (including that of advocacy groups, the organisation and donors) are all worth considering (Magee, 2007).

Regardless of the presentation format, an evaluation output needs to present essential information, which includes the background, context, methods, findings, discussion and recommendations, and conclusion. Differences occur in the medium, detail and language style, rather than in the content.

Whatever format is chosen – and usually it will be more than one – the practitioner needs to take into account the following:

- Will this format impinge on any ethical issues surrounding evaluation participants' confidentiality and anonymity?
- Is this format aligned to the context and aims of the service and its evaluation?
- How complex is the evaluation and can it be accurately conveyed in this format?
- To what kind of format is this particular audience most likely to be receptive?

## Writing style

A written evaluation output – in whatever format – needs to be succinct and to the point. The writing needs to present practical and factual information in a straightforward and simple way, avoiding jargon, complex writing or literary verbosity. The readers need to be kept in mind when drafting the outputs. This means considering what they might already know, need to know, what might surprise them, annoy or interest them. Members of the local community, politicians, policy makers, the service's board of management, other arts & health practitioners, funders or a senior management team will each have distinctive biases and discourses. The writing style needs to take the audience into account in order to communicate findings most effectively.

While multiple formats of reporting use different kinds of language (e.g. formal, informal, professional or colloquial), they need to convey the same information. Given the complexities of most organisations, diplomacy ensures that not too many feathers are ruffled and that the evaluation recommendations are acted upon. Here it is crucial for practitioners to ensure that they are up to date with current language and terminology within the organisation, and that they are as informed as possible of diplomatic complications. For example, while the term 'impact' has become a key term in the policy-making and funding world, and is often associated with evaluation of services, many arts-based practitioners shy away from its implications, preferring to consider the focus of practice to be process and experience.

## 5.2 Structuring evaluation reports

Whatever their output format, evaluation reports tend to follow similar sequential conventions in terms of content. A template covering all sections that are expected to appear in a standard written report helps to structure the evaluation findings, even when it is the output format and the audience that determines the amount and depth of information.

A full written evaluation report generally contains the following sections:

1. cover page
2. acknowledgements
3. table of contents
4. summary
5. background and context
6. evaluation framework
7. findings
8. discussion
9. conclusions
10. references
11. appendices.

The logic of these sections may apply in other evaluation outputs, such as slide-show presentations.

### (1) Cover page

The cover page is the reader's first impression and should clearly communicate what the document is about. It includes the project title, subtitle, relevant names, report date, sponsors, institutional logos and, importantly, the fact that it is an evaluation report, rather than a project proposal or funding application. The title needs to be descriptive of the project, while keeping the targeted audience in mind.

## (2) Acknowledgments

Thanking people involved in the evaluation goes a long way to generating goodwill and trust, although it may be prudent to check whether or not they want to be named. Those thanked can include funders, managers, colleagues, respondents, external players such as a funding body, and anyone whose contribution was significant for the project, such as the service users who gave their time and opinion. Acknowledgments can equally be at the end of the report.

## (3) Table of contents

This includes section titles, sub-section titles and page numbers, which help to navigate through the report quickly. It is crucial that the page numbers are correct!

## (4) Summary

Providing a summary or snapshot report of the project findings is good practice, especially when the report is addressed to readers (such as funders, managers and policy makers) who may have limited time to read a long and detailed report. No more than three pages long, with sub-headings and bullet points to break up the text and increase readability, the summary includes only crucial information and the main evaluation findings, using exactly the same subheadings as the full report with pages numbers next to each heading showing where the full section is located in the report.

## *(5) Background and context*

This introductory section sets the organisational context for the service being evaluated, including the geographical, socioeconomic, political, environmental and historical context and setting as necessary. This section is often omitted by internal evaluators who assume that readers have this information. However, including the organisational context for the evaluation project and a full description of the service allows readers who are not familiar with the intricacies of a service to be able to have a good understanding of it.

Providing a clear background and context for the evaluation is critical to understanding its rationale. This section usually includes the following:

- *organisational information:* information about the organisation's ethos, history, location and purpose

- *background of the service:* information about the service provision, including its aims and development, the different formats and service user groups to which it is provided and its funding arrangements.

The background and context section can include supporting documentation, such as photos of examples of work, programmes and press cuttings. Alternatively, these may be included in the appendices and only referenced in this section. In larger reports, this section may include brief information about existing research evidence in the field that draws from relevant literature.

## *(6) Evaluation framework*

This section usually provides information concerning:

- *evaluation aims:* these need to show why the evaluation took place, and how its aims link to the service aims

- *evaluation timeline:* overview of the different evaluation phases and their timings

- *collection methods:* description of the evaluation tools and the participants (including a description of sample recruitment procedures)
- *analysis methods:* description of how evaluation data and material was processed.

The information provided in this section helps the reader to judge how systematic the evaluation has been and how robust and reliable the findings are likely to be.

## (7) Findings

Findings represent more than the collected 'raw' data. Findings not only report on facts deriving from the quantitative and qualitative data, but also contextualise these facts with relevant commentary. The data, for example, may show that 36 people attended the evaluation focus groups. Reporting the findings, however, may provide a wider frame. For example: 'The evaluation focus group did not attract as many participants as planned. Thirty-six people attended compared with the original target of 60 project participants. The timing clash of external activities with the evaluation focus group reduced the attendance of project participants.'

A detailed profile of the evaluation participants (e.g. numbers and characteristics) should also be provided in the findings. It needs to be clear which participant group (e.g. service users, staff or management) provided what kind of data.

Whether in a full written report, a conference poster, less formal presentation or slide-show format, the findings need to make links between the evaluation aims and objectives, the data analysis and the evaluation conclusions and recommendations. In presenting the findings, economy and efficiency of information are paramount. Numeric data is often presented as tables, pie charts or graphs, while narrative data can be thematically summarised. Quotations illustrate key findings and allow participants' voices to be heard.

Reports need to present the evaluation findings honestly and accurately, regardless of whether findings report positive or negative impact. Negative findings are often a vehicle for improvement and development of the service. It is often these findings that are likely to highlight areas where the service is not fulfilling its aims, or where ideas for innovative practices can emerge. Although it can be difficult for practitioners to see their service criticised, by presenting the full range of evaluative responses to a project or service, practitioners ensure credibility on the basis of robust and unbiased evaluation methods.

## *(8) Discussion*

Having presented the findings, the discussion allows for speculation and critique, both situating the findings within the service and also reframing them through the broader agendas of its commissioners, project stakeholders, evaluation participants, service users and professional bodies. This section also alerts the reader to the limits of the evaluation, including, for example, the small number of evaluation participants. By pointing out both the strengths and weaknesses of the evaluation process, the reader is invited to trust that information is not be withheld in the report, however unwelcome it might be.

Recommendations – a crucial part of the discussion – help identify what aspects of the service need to be addressed on the basis of the evaluation aims and findings. On the basis of service 'success', this section can recommend that some aspects be maintained or expanded; other findings may lead to recommendations of change, where it seems necessary, and what kind of change might be the most efficient. Recommendations may also consider the impact of findings on funding, organisational resources, the work team and organisation, and for those beyond the organisation (e.g. policy makers, advocacy groups and local councillors). Depending on the evaluation brief, each recommendation can also be accompanied by identifying suggested action points.

## *(9) Conclusions*

This short section summarises and reinforces the main 'messages' of the evaluation. On the basis of the discussion and recommendations, the conclusions reinforce the impact of the service, how the service might be improved and who might benefit from such improvements or changes. In brief reports, conclusions may well be integrated as part of the discussion and do not form a separate section.

## *(10) References*

Any references to existing literature and evidence that are made in the evaluation report need to be fully cited. Using a clear citation style helps readers to easily follow up any references they are interested in. There are many styles of referencing to choose from (e.g. the Harvard or the American Psychological Association citation style), but the most important factor is to keep reference lists consistent – in other words, to use the same reference style throughout. Details about different citation styles are easily accessible online.

## *(11) Appendices*

These include any information that, if included earlier, would interrupt the flow of the main report. Often, they include examples of blank evaluation tools (e.g. questionnaires, log-sheets, interview questions) and any other supporting information (e.g. initial evaluation proposal) that shows how the evaluation was conducted. In addition, the following can be included:

- practitioners' biographical note and photograph
- detailed figures illustrating the collection/analysis methods and/or the findings
- press cuttings
- examples of work, including CDs/DVDs with audio-visual recordings
- budget details.

## Labelling figures

Every figure (including tables, charts, graphs, diagrams and photographs) should be numbered sequentially, labelled clearly and positioned as close to the relevant text as possible. For each figure it is critical to:

- Provide a title and a caption with a number (e.g. 'Figure 1 Number of children accessing individual and group music therapy sessions'). The title needs to be able to stand alone. Similarly axis labels are needed to indicate what the values on each axis (e.g. the vertical and horizontal axes) refer to. This is so that anyone reading this specific diagram out of context can understand what it means. Titles of figures need to be brief but informative. If necessary, explanatory notes can be added under the table or figure.

- Make appropriate use of colours to enhance readability. For example, the bar with the number of 'No' answers and the bar with the number of 'Yes' answers can be identified by using red and green respectively. Also, it is worth considering whether readers will receive colour-printed or black-and-white copies of the report. In the latter case, it might be more appropriate to use different patterns (dots, stripes, etc.) instead of colours.

## Referring to figures

Figures not only need to be labelled but also need to be cross-referred in the main text of the evaluation report. Suggestions include:

- Making specific reference to each figure. It cannot be assumed that the reader will make the necessary connection between the text and the figure, especially if the layout of the page means that the figure does not appear near to the relevant text.

- Referring to each figure in the text by its specific number (i.e. avoid writing 'the figure above/below/on the next page').

- Remembering to guide the reader to interpreting the information in the figure. What does the figure show? What specific point is being made? What are the most important points to notice in this figure?

The box below provides a list with examples showing commonly used ways of cross-referring and commenting upon figures.

As shown in Figure 1 below, over 50 per cent of the people who have accessed the music therapy service during the evaluation period have learning disabilities.

The mean number of cancellations of music therapy sessions per school term is shown in Figure 2.

The majority of staff (88%) suggest that music therapy impacts positively on the general atmosphere of the hospital (see Figure 3).

## Proof-reading and drafts

The full evaluation report needs to be proof-read, and amendments inserted as it is developed. It is also advisable to make time for sending the full document to other people to check it with fresh eyes, which adds to the timeframe for producing the final version of the report, but ultimately enhances the accuracy and professionalism of the final document. Involving an external person to check the documents for errors needs to be planned well ahead of time in order to synchronise respective timeframes and diaries.

It is also important to inform other partner organisations about any negative findings to which they may be sensitive before the document is sent out. It is important to phrase criticisms of any organisational issues in a way that is not offensive and in a way that it is shown as something that can be changed for the better. Involving relevant stakeholders as much as possible at this stage creates a sense of shared ownership of the evaluation and is less likely to lead to unwelcome surprises.

### *Common pitfalls of written reports*

The most common weakness of evaluation reports is the inclusion of too much description of the background, context and methods, and not enough space for findings, discussion and recommendations.

While compiling the report, the audience and commissioners need to be kept in mind constantly, and the report 'voice' should remain consistent. Findings need to be presented in ways that are congruent with evaluation aims, the organisational context and the nature of the service.

Brief and succinct passages of text, interspersed with tables and bullet points, and the use of photographs and diagrams help to reduce report length and make the report visually engaging.

# Phase 6

## Finalising and Disseminating Outputs

### 6.1 Design, formatting and layout

Clear presentation and thoughtful design enhances the impact of evaluation outputs. Effective design and layout of a document increases the report's readability and ultimately ensures that information is efficiently communicated.

There are certain rules that increase the visual appeal of a document. If the document is too long, does not present any illustrations and is only text, the reader will struggle to engage with the document and digest all the information given. Readers usually flip through the document to see how it is structured; if it has images, figures and varying styles and formats, readers will be more likely to engage with it.

The following tips ensure that the 'look' of a document is representative of the quality of the work.

### Layout

Clear and consistent titles and subtitles enhance any document. Subtitles help to break up paragraphs and guide readers through the document with greater ease.

Blank, white space in a document may feel wasteful, but allowing enough space between sections helps readers to engage with the text and avoid information overload.

The text layout can be changed from one section to another – for example, from one column to two, or to text flowing around images. These changes make visual distinctions between sections and engage readers' attention.

Bullet points convey information succinctly and efficiently, preventing clutter and overload. They help readers to skim-read more accurately, and draw readers' attention effectively to important points of information.

## Fonts

The choice of font needs to suits the style and image that the report wants to portray. The fonts used need to be consistent. One or two fonts are sufficient for most documents – for example, one font for the main body text, and one for titles and subtitles. Consistency of fonts and sizes gives a clean, professional finish to the document.

Font size 12 is generally regarded as the standard size for body text because it is large enough to read, yet small enough to look neat. Smaller fonts can be used in charts and tables, and also in the labelling of diagrams and charts. This distinguishes labelling from the regular body text, allowing the eye to identify the various sections. Titles and subtitles should appear as larger font sizes, or perhaps underlined or in bold. Whatever method is chosen to define certain parts of text from others, it needs to be consistent throughout the document. It is worth checking organisational guidelines in terms of font types, sizes and colour schemes.

## Colours

The use of colours (e.g. for defining fonts, headers, boxes) can make a report much more accessible and engaging. However, use of colour should be applied appropriately and sparingly for maximum impact. Most organisations with a strong brand or image associate particular colours with their brand. It is worth checking with the organisation's communications department the official colours that may be used in the evaluation report. If unconstrained by organisational colours, then these should be limited to a certain palette of colours per report in order to provide a unified and professional finish.

FIGURE 23 TWO EXAMPLES OF EVALUATION REPORT PAGE LAYOUTS

Session numbers were reduced between 13th and 27th June 2012 as the wards, in which the open group is conducted, were closed due to a viral outbreak for three consecutive weeks. Also, no sessions took place on 7th June 2012 due to music therapist's annual leave.

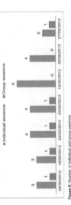

Figure 6: Number of individual and group sessions

## C. Reported experiences of music therapy[3]

### Benefits to children (patients)

All children (patients) who completed a questionnaire report that they like doing music with the music therapist.

No negative feedback is given by the children. According to them, the only aspect of music therapy that they do not like is that their session is "too short" or "has to end".

One child mentioned that they enjoy group sessions best because they get to play with other children.

All children report that playing instruments and/or singing is their favourite thing about music therapy. Two children report they like "making lots of noise". Other responses are: "watching other children play", "trying to beat the drum to the rhythm" and "choosing songs".

*He never seen him like that before. He was really concentrating and following what was going on. It was fantastic! It walks about to find something he really responds to. I've never heard of music therapy before – I'll see if I can find some locally.*

Mother of a 0-9 year old with Haemophilia and ASD

In alignment with children's statements, parents' and staff's/volunteers' questionnaire responses suggest that music therapy (MT) offers a variety of benefits (see Table 3).

---

[3] The outcomes presented in sections C, D and E originate from questionnaire responses and narrative feedback. Quotes are taken from music therapist's log-sheet and Nordoff Robbins's website www.nordoff-robbins.org.uk

---

# OUTCOMES

The evaluation outcomes are structured in five main sections:

A. Profile of evaluation participants
B. Audit of music therapy access
C. Reported experiences of music therapy
D. The impact and role of music therapy at the centre
E. Suggestions for development of the music therapy service

## A. Profile of evaluation participants

A total of 26 people responded to the questionnaire (Figure 1):

- 14 service-users (54%)
- 9 staff (34%)
- 2 family members and friends (8%)
- 1 music therapist (4%)

- Service-users
- Staff
- Family members/friends
- Music therapist

Figure 1: Evaluation participants

50% of the service-users who responded to the evaluation questionnaire have attended in excess of 10 sessions (Figure 2) something that enables them to have well-informed opinions about the service. Some service-users have taken part in music therapy in more than one format, i.e. attending both individual and group sessions.

All staff members who completed questionnaires have experienced music therapy either through participation or by observing sessions. However, family members and friends had indirect experience of music therapy, drawing on feedback from their relative/friend (service-user).

- 1-4 sessions
- 5-9 sessions
- 10 sessions or more
- Not sure
- None

Figure 2: Number of music therapy sessions attended by service-users

It is also important to consider whether the report will be photocopier-friendly. Will the colours still be distinguishable in black and white? Particularly when labelling bar charts with several different colours, it will be important to be able to distinguish between the bar colours even when it is printed in black and white. A test print-run will help to check this.

## Figures

It is important that there is not too much writing in the report and that the report can be understood quickly and easily. Here, visuals are helpful if used carefully and strategically (Figure 23). Graphics, snapshots, tables and charts all enhance communication of information. However, a report can be less effective if it is visually overloaded with figures (including tables, diagrams and graphs). Figures that are not presented clearly can create confusion and be misinterpreted by the reader.

## Boxes

Boxes that separate some text from the main body text can highlight main findings or direct quotations from evaluation participants, break up a long piece of prose and make the report easier to engage with. This is a technique that newspaper and magazine editors use to communicate the main points of an article or key phrases by drawing readers' interest and therefore enticing them to read more thoroughly. The most representative quotations can be highlighted using this method.

## Images

A picture tells a thousand words... Not only does a photograph break up the text and make a document more visually appealing, but photographs of people in action offer valuable evidence of the service. However, photographs must have the necessary level and kind of written informed consent for their use; in addition, they need to be relevant to the surrounding text.

### Logos and headed paper

At times, reports need to be produced on an organisation's headed paper. Even if this is not the case, it is a good idea to use the logo of the organisation and any partner organisations who are heavily involved in the evaluation project and/or the arts-based service provision. These are placed either on every page or simply on the front cover.

### Binding

If a hard copy of the evaluation report is being produced, it needs to be properly bound. This is an important finishing touch, since it allows the reader to read and turn pages easily as well as enjoy the feel of a professional document. Using staples looks unprofessional and spoils the feel of the report.

The time and expenditure needed for printing, binding and disseminating (as outlined below) an evaluation report should not be underestimated.

## 6.2 Methods of dissemination

Depending upon the organisational culture and the requirements of the evaluation commissioners and audience, electronic copies or upload of the report to a website may be expected in addition to printed and bound hard copies. It is critical to explore all possible avenues for ensuring appropriate and efficient ways of passing the report to the intended readers.

If distributing hard copies of the report, ensure that an appropriate means of getting the document to the receiver has been identified (e.g. post, staff pigeonhole, desks). Scenarios where a report has been lost or gone unaccounted for through inadequate means of distribution are not rare.

If an electronic copy of the evaluation document is being emailed, it needs to be in a PDF format (or any other secure electronic format), so that the layout and content cannot be altered. It is also important to ensure that the receiver is aware of any potential circulation restrictions; the report should only be circulated to the intended audiences. The report is likely to contain sensitive information and therefore should only be circulated to approved persons.

If the organisation wishes the document to be uploaded to a website, copyright clauses and other legal rights need to be in place. These are explained below in Section 6.4, 'Online availability, intellectual property and copyrights'.

Depending on the aim and scale of the evaluation, the organisation's communication or fundraising department could organise a press release; this could help communication of the evaluation findings to a wider audience. The different stakeholders, however, need to liaise carefully so that the evaluation findings are communicated clearly and accurately, since the language used for promotion and fundraising purposes at times can be at odds with the language used for evaluation purposes.

## 6.3 Evaluation posters and leaflets

Findings will generally be circulated via a written report, but it may also be appropriate to communicate them via a presentation or through posters and/or leaflets that can be displayed in an entrance hall, ward or staff room (see Figure 24). This may be one of the only ways that the evaluation participants (e.g. staff members, patients, residents and family members) are able to see the outcome of their participation in an evaluation. Creating an accessible leaflet targeted specifically at evaluation participants is also a respectful way of communicating appreciation for their participation in the evaluation project. The design, formatting and layout considerations outlined earlier are also applicable to posters. Brevity and visual engagement are the key factors.

**NORDOFF ROBBINS**
music transforming lives

Music therapy at [organisation]:
## SUMMARY OF EVALUATION FINDINGS

### BACKGROUND

Nordoff Robbins has provided music therapy at [organisation] since 1994. Music therapist Nicky O'Neill gives sessions to individual children and groups every Wednesday.

Music therapy aims to support children both emotionally and developmentally during their admission. Also, it provides opportunities for children, parents and staff to interact and socialise through music-making.

Using questionnaires and interviews, Nordoff Robbins carried out an evaluation (May-July 2012) to find out children's, parents' and staff's perceptions of what the music therapy service offers at [organisation] and how it can develop.

*"I've never seen him like that before. He was really concentrating and following what you were doing. It was fantastic! It's really good to find something he really responds to. I've never heard of music therapy before – I'll see if I can find some locally."*
**Mother of a child with leukaemia and autism**

### FINDINGS

A total of 77 people (including staff, parents and children) took part in the evaluation. 31 sessions took place and 141 attendances were logged during the 7-week evaluation period.

#### WHAT DID THE CHILDREN SAY?
All children say that they like doing music with the music therapist and they look forward to it every week.

#### WHAT DID PARENTS SAY?
Parents say that they value music therapy as a fun and interactive activity which is something 'normal' for their children to get involved in and which can boost their children's confidence. Music therapy can provide both them and their children with emotional support in what can be a stressful hospital environment. Parents say that music therapy alleviates their anxiety and helps them to interact with their children in a stimulating and creative way.

*"Music therapy is the only activity I have seen that allows parents and children to interact in a relaxed atmosphere; for mutual benefit."*
**Father of a child with leukaemia**

#### WHAT DID STAFF SAY?
Staff say that music therapy offers peer support, reduces depression, tension and anger, and gives children another way to communicate without words. Many staff members suggest that music therapy provides a useful way of working with children and offers them a different view of the children. They also report that music therapy affects their mood positively and gives staff the opportunity to observe the children enjoying themselves.

*"My child couldn't talk much and had stopped talking altogether as she was obviously in pain. The music provided a way for her to indicate how she was feeling and seemed to take away some anxiety about being in hospital."*
**Mother of a child with liver tumour**

### IN GENERAL...

Most evaluation participants report that music therapy lifts the mood in the hospital and increases interaction between people. 82% of staff members report that music therapy makes the atmosphere of the hospital more relaxed and 67% report that it increases interaction between people. The wish for continuation and expansion of the service is a common request by the participants, suggesting that the collaboration between Nordoff Robbins and [organisation] is a worthwhile investment.

For further information, please contact [name of person], Head of Music Services for Inner London
Nordoff Robbins, 2 Lissenden Gardens, London NW5 1PQ    Email: [name]@nordoff-robbins.org.uk Tel: +44 (0)20 7267 4496

FIGURE 24 A LEAFLET CREATED FOR INFORMING PARTICIPANTS
ABOUT THE FINDINGS OF AN EVALUATION PROJECT

## 6.4 Online availability, intellectual property and copyrights

In the UK, intellectual products such as evaluation reports are protected under the Copyright, Designs and Patents Act 1988. Similar laws exist in other countries. Copyright can be summarised as an automatic right which arises whenever an individual or company creates a product, document or work (The UK Copyright Service, 2009). However, copyright law was developed before the advances in information technology. With the rise of the internet, the ability to enforce, notify and attribute copyright has become problematic. A piece of work can be officially uploaded on one site and replicated on multiple sites without the consent or knowledge of the creator.

Restricting the availability of online products would be problematic and arguably damaging to the organisation. The internet offers cheap and extensive means for the dissemination of products, including evaluation findings. Such organisational profiling is a vital component for private, public and third sector activity in the age of the internet. It is within this context that the Creative Commons licences were developed.

Like the copyright mark (i.e. ©), Creative Commons licences are a clear public means for expressing the ownership of a creation. These licences allow any individual or organisation to grant copyright permissions to their creative work, including evaluation reports when uploaded online.

Various organisations are committed to some intellectual products being freely available on the internet. However, in the interests of their integrity and brand, it is worthwhile to take steps to protect the intellectual property of products (such as evaluation reports) created under the name of the organisation.

There are several Creative Commons licences which correspond to the various levels of free use a creator may wish to place on their work. *Attribution Non-Commercial No Derivative (CC BY-NC-ND)* is the most restrictive licence. This allows a work to be copied and shared with others, but only in its original form, for non-commercial purposes and where credit is provided to the original author.

Generally speaking, Attribution Non-Commercial No Derivative (CC BY-NC-ND) is the most appropriate licence when publishing an evaluation report for the following reasons:

- It allows quick, free and open dissemination but ensures credit, that no commercial gain will be made through the use of the evaluation report and that the report will be kept intact – it cannot be built upon or changed.

- It is arguably easier for an organisation to make a transition from a restrictive to more open use dissemination.

Creative Commons licences are not an alternative to copyright but have been individually developed for compatibility with the legal framework of each country in which they are active. Creators do not give up their copyright when a Creative Commons licence is created for a product – a licence depends on copyright law. Without copyright, the permission for the level of use expressed within a licence would be meaningless and ineffective. Therefore, any rights that are expressed and granted through licensing can only be made in addition to those already present in copyright law.

Even though licences are non-revocable, many organisations still see benefits in the use of licences. The take up of licences has been greatest within the public and not-for-profit sectors (Coats, 2007). All licences can be obtained by the creators free of charge from the Creative Commons website (www.creativecommons.org) and the licences permit access to online material free of charge.

Phase 6 does not denote the end of the evaluation journey. As the phases diagram in the Introduction (Figure 2) suggested evaluation is an ongoing cycle. Although the positioning of 'A Note on Ethics' in the next section seems to suggest that ethical considerations happen after Phase 6, considering the safety of all participants needs to inform all six evaluation phases.

# A Note on Ethics

Broadly speaking, research studies always require ethical review, while audits, evaluation and monitoring projects generally do not (see Table 1). However, the lines between what constitutes evaluation and what constitutes research can at times be unclear, and labelling is not necessarily consistent across all practices and organisations. In any case, Wade (2005, p.468) warns that 'decisions about the need for ethical review should be based on the morality of all actions rather than arbitrary distinctions between audit and research'.

Although evaluation projects most often do not require the approval of a Research Ethics Committee (see Table 1), practitioners are responsible for designing and conducting an ethically informed and sound evaluation. This brief chapter outlines some basic ethical principles and procedures that need to be considered. Practitioners who wish to find out more about ethics, including substantial details concerning the development of both participant information sheets and informed consent forms, are encouraged to read *A Guide to Research Ethics for Arts Therapists and Arts & Health Practitioners* (Farrant, Pavlicevic and Tsiris, 2014).

## Laws, legislations and policies

Sensitivity to the ethical complexities of evaluation that involves vulnerable people is important and relies on familiarity with the relevant legislation, such as the UK's Mental Capacity Act 2005. Most organisations have policies and procedures that address and alert staff to such complexities. Having an understanding of the organisation's infrastructure helps practitioners to check whether their evaluation complies with the organisational research governance framework, and whether all managing and reporting lines are in place. This understanding helps to detect and prevent any potential misconduct, and clarifies people's diverse roles within the evaluation team. Having a complaints procedure in place and ensuring transparency of the evaluation design and procedures are always important. Even if ethical review is not required (as is often the case with evaluations), practitioners are encouraged to discuss this with the research ethics representative of their organisation to find out more about the ethical implications of conducting an evaluation project.

### Safeguarding evaluation participants

Participants' dignity, rights, safety and wellbeing need to be safeguarded throughout the evaluation process; practitioners have to think carefully about the benefits and risks that people's involvement may entail. For example, conducting evaluations with vulnerable people who experience serious illnesses and have a limited life expectancy brings a range of ethical (and practical) complexities which are not to be underestimated (Dileo, 2005). Practitioners, for example, need to think carefully about the ethical justification of asking terminally ill and often dependent patients to participate in studies, especially when it may require extra time and effort on their behalf (Tsiris and Hartley, 2013).

### Data storage

In all cases, practitioners need to think carefully how participants' privacy, confidentiality and anonymity can be protected throughout the evaluation process. Evaluation data should be stored securely and safely according to the laws of data protection (e.g. the UK's Data Protection Act 1998).

### Participant information sheets and consent forms

Although it is a legal requirement for *research* that involves human beings to obtain written informed consent, for evaluation participants it is not always an organisational requirement (Farrant, Pavlicevic and Tsiris, 2014). Whether or not written informed consent is a prerequisite, however, evaluators need to take into account and communicate to participants their rights, including their right to not participate or to withdraw from the evaluation.

This information can be communicated through a specifically designed participant information sheet which is accompanied by a relevant consent form where participants can signal whether or not they wish to take part. In some cases, participant information sheets and consent forms are integrated into one single document, whereas, in other cases, the information usually included in a participant information sheet and consent form can be integrated in the actual evaluation tool. The latter is often the case with questionnaires and surveys, where a brief opening paragraph communicates all the necessary information.

In all cases, evaluation participants need to be informed about certain issues, including the evaluation aim, what the participants' role entails, any participation-related benefits and risks, the right to opt in or out, the right to withdraw, what will be done with participants' responses, whether and how confidentiality, anonymity and privacy are maintained, and, finally, how participants can ask any questions and voice any concerns or complaints about the evaluation.

Tips for writing participant information sheets and consent forms include:

- use of clear, ordinary language rather than technical terms or buzz words
- short sentences that are as concise as possible
- avoidance of intimidating or coercive phrases such as 'You understand that...' or 'You have been told that...'
- writing in the second person – for example, 'You are invited to participate in an evaluation of the art therapy service at Beachford Hospital'
- use of the active rather than passive voice, since these sound more personal and current – for example, 'We decided' rather than 'It was decided'
- avoidance of small print and the use of unclear fonts.

## Mental capacity and 'grateful participants'

Obtaining consent for participation can be a challenge when potential participants' conditions prevent them from having the mental capacity to consent in writing, or indeed consent for themselves at all. In such cases, additional procedures may be necessary; see, for example, the procedures required by the Mental Capacity Act 2005 (Farrant, Pavlicevic and Tsiris, 2014).

Also, practitioners occasionally come across cases of 'grateful participants' whose gratitude for the service, or their sense of vulnerability, prevents them from being honest in their responses or refusing to participate in an evaluation. In such cases, it is important to reassure participants that their participation will have no impact on their access to the service.

# Conclusion

Not evaluating is not an option.

Experienced sailors in the Arctic Circle know that (shrinking) icebergs are tips of vast invisible underwater structures. This book has sought to alert practitioners to the evaluation iceberg – especially the invisible concealed bits – by providing the equivalent of a scuba diving kit and deep-diving training. Whatever the temperature, the visibility and scale of concealments, we hope to have persuaded you of essential fundamentals: a critical, questioning attitude coupled with a range of systematic procedures, together with that imaginative flexibility that is at the heart of artistic practices. All of this while also remaining alert for, and intrigued by, unexpected events, discursive currents, unpredictable professional and organisational climates, and the inevitable pressures of advocacy, funding and politics. There are also the invisible and inevitable trip wires: people dynamics and relationships, histories of suspicion, friendships, and even infatuations that intersect carefully laid evaluation plans with exasperating predictability.

Rather like icebergs, evaluation reports conceal more than they reveal. The report is the product of weeks, if not months, of planning, assembling and refining all kinds of materials and information, drawn from within and around organisational structures from people in different roles and hats; information about practices, and project outputs such as paintings, poems, performances and funny clowns. Our hope is that the phases in this guide offer a radar as well as a practical toolkit for harvesting information systematically, at the right time, from the right persons, and for accompanying you right through to producing the visible tip of all that hard work.

Evaluation reports do not simply speak to practitioners or service users: the creative challenge is to speak convincingly to audiences that hold different, and at times colliding, understandings of what constitutes evidence and what evidence is effective. Throughout the guide we have emphasised the need for practitioners to remain committed to the core values of arts-based practices and to people's experiences, while also engaging vigorously with the necessity of systematic and robust representation of evidence – in whatever forms. It is the tensions between these disparate values that we all need to enter and work with, rather than being tempted to dismiss one set of values at the cost of others, at the behest of external pressures.

We have not sought to steer you towards a single value system. Having considered the procedures and questions in this guide, and imagined these through the prism of your practices and projects, our hope is that your enthusiasm and impatience have risen steadily, and that you feel ready to ask the right kinds of questions, in many different ways, and have the confidence to assemble different types of information, on the bases of multiple agendas and values.

Finally, unpredictability is at the very core of the arts – and artists of all persuasions know that so-called 'mistakes' open doors: a 'wrong' note or 'smudge' propels a work of art towards other unexpected dimensions. By their very nature, the arts thrive on the rigours of the unknown, on flexibility and imagination, on meticulous attention to practicalities, and on connecting us with one another in time and place. Artistic practices are built on painstaking craftsmanship and technical skill, and on the capacity to absorb all kinds of paradoxes: the unpredictable and systematic, the aesthetic and the outcome measures, the ephemeral and economic. As artists well know, asymmetries and tensions push us towards the edges where creativity and new works thrive. Evaluation, we suggest, can be uncomfortably creative and unpredictably interesting.

Good luck!

# References

Aldridge, D. (2005a) 'Guidelines for Case Study Design Research in Music Therapy.' In D. Aldridge (ed.) *Case Study Designs in Music Therapy*. London: Jessica Kingsley Publishers.

Aldridge, D. (2005b) 'A Story Told from Practice: The Reflective Inquirer in an Ecology of Ideas.' In D. Aldridge (ed.) *Case Study Designs in Music Therapy*. London: Jessica Kingsley Publishers.

Aldridge, G. (2005) 'Therapeutic Narrative Analysis as a Narrative Case Study Approach.' In D. Aldridge (ed.) *Case Study Designs in Music Therapy*. London: Jessica Kingsley Publishers.

Ansdell, G. and Pavlicevic, M. (2001) *Beginning Research in the Arts Therapies: A Practical Guide*. London: Jessica Kingsley Publishers.

Antonovsky, A. (1996) 'The salutogenic model as a theory to guide health promotion.' *Health Promotion International 11*, 1, 11–18.

Armstrong, R. (1987) 'The midpoint on a five-point Likert-type scale.' *Perceptual and Motor Skills 64*, 359–362.

Ball, J. and Shanks, A. (2012) 'Gaining feedback from people with learning disabilities.' *British Journal of Occupational Therapy 75*, 10, 471–477.

Bristol-Myers Squibb Foundation (undated) 'Step 6: Monitor and Evaluate.' Available at www.bms.com/documents/STF/manual/step_6.pdf, accessed on 1 March 2013.

Coats, J. (2007) 'Creative Commons – The Next Generation: Creative Commons licence use five years on.' *SCRIPTed 4*, 1. Available at www.law.ed.ac.uk/ahrc/script-ed/vol4-1/coates.asp, accessed on 29 July 2013.

Coupe O'Kane, J. and Goldbart, J. (1998) *Communication before Speech: Development and Assessment*. London: David Fulton Publishers.

Daykin, N. (2007) 'Context, Culture and Risk: Towards an Understanding of the Impact of Music in Health Care Settings.' In J. Edwards (ed.) *Music: Promoting Health and Creating Community in Healthcare Contexts*. Newcastle: Cambridge Scholar Publishing.

Dileo, C. (2005) 'Ethical Precautions in Music Therapy Research.' In B. Wheeler (ed.) *Music Therapy Research* (2nd Edition). Gilsum, NH: Barcelona Publishers.

Dorman, P.J., Slattery, J., Farrell, B., Dennis, M.S. and Sandercock, P.A.G. (1997) 'A randomised comparison of the EuroQol and Short Form-36 after stroke: United Kingdom collaborators in the International Stroke Trial.' *British Medical Journal 315*, 7106, 461.

Edwards, A. and Talbot, R. (1999) *The Hard-Pressed Researcher: A Research Handbook for the Caring Professions*. Essex: Pearson Education.

Farrant, C., Pavlicevic, M. and Tsiris, G. (2014) *A Guide to Research Ethics for Arts Therapists and Arts & Health Practitioners.* London: Jessica Kingsley Publishers.

Feuerstein, M. (1986) *Partners in Evaluation: Evaluating Development and Community Programmes with Participants.* London: Macmillan.

French, R. (2001) "Negative capability': managing the confusing uncertainties of change.' *Journal of Organizational Change Management 14,* 5, 480–492.

Gold, C., Rolvsjord, R. Mössler, K. and Stige, B. (2013) 'Reliability and validity of a scale to measure interest in music among clients in mental health care.' *Psychology of Music 41,* 5, 665–682.

HCPC (Health and Care Professions Council) (2013) Standards of Proficiency – Arts Therapists. Available at www.hpc-uk.org/publications/standards/index. asp?id=39, accessed on 21 July 2013.

Hedrick, T.E. (1994) 'The Quantitative-Qualitative Debate: Possibilities for Integration.' In C.S. Reichardt and S.F. Rallis (eds) *The Qualitative-Quantitative Debate: New Perspectives.* San Francisco, CA: Jossey-Bass Publishers.

Higgins, R. (1993) *Approaches to Case Study: A Handbook for Those Entering the Field.* London: Jessica Kingsley Publishers.

Jones, P. (2012) 'Approaches to the futures of research (Based on the conference keynote, British Association of Dramatherapists Conference 2011, *Measure for measures, researching, re-viewing and re-framing dramatherapy in practice*).' *Dramatherapy 34,* 2, 63–82.

Jones, P. and Dokter, D. (2012) 'Dramatherapy vignette research: What are children in therapy.' Keynote presentation at the conference Music Therapy and Dramatherapy with Children in Educational and Other Settings, Anglia Ruskin University, 1 December 2012.

Karkou, V. (2010) 'Summary and Conclusions.' In V. Karkou (ed.) *Arts Therapies in Schools: Research and Practice.* London: Jessica Kingsley Publishers.

Kusek, J.Z. and Rist, R. (2004) *Handbook for Development Practitioners: Ten Steps to a Results-Based Monitoring and Evaluation System.* Washington, DC: International Bank for Reconstruction and Development/World Bank.

Lawes, M. (2012) 'Reporting on outcomes: an adaptation of the 'AQR-instrument' used to evaluate music therapy in autism.' *Approaches: Music Therapy & Special Music Education 4,* 2, 110–120. Available at http://approaches.primarymusic.gr/ approaches/journal/Approaches_4(2)_2012/Approaches_4(2)2012_Lawes_Article.pdf, accessed on 3 July 2013.

Magee, W. (2007) 'Focussing on Outcomes: Undertaking the Music Therapy Research Journey in Medical Settings.' In J. Edwards (ed.) *Music: Promoting Health and Creating Community in Healthcare Contexts.* Newcastle: Cambridge Scholar Publishing.

North, F. (2011) *From Pre-Intentional to Intentional Communication: Exploring Speech and Language Therapy Concepts and Assessments for Music Therapy with Children with Severe, Profound and Multiple Learning Disabilities.* Unpublished MMT dissertation, Nordoff Robbins, London.

OECD (Organisation for Economic Co-operation and Development) (2002) *Glossary of Key Terms in Evaluation and Results-Based Management.* Paris: OECD/DAC.

Procter, S. (2002) 'Empowering and Enabling: Music Therapy in Non-Medical Mental Health Provision.' In C. Kenny and B. Stige (eds) *Contemporary Voices in Music Therapy.* Oslo: Unipub Forlag.

Raw, A., Lewis, S., Russell, A. and Macnaughton, J. (2012) 'A hole in the heart: confronting the drive for evidence-based impact research in arts and health.' *Arts & Health 4,* 2, 97–108.

Robson, C. (2002) *Real World Research: A Resource for Social Scientists and Practitioner-Researchers.* Oxford: Blackwell.

Rolvsjord, R. (2004) 'Therapy as empowerment: clinical and political implications of empowerment philosophy in mental health practices of music therapy.' *Nordic Journal of Music Therapy 13*, 2, 99–111.

Sale, J.E., Lohfeld, L.H. and Brazil, K. (2002) 'Revisiting the quantitative-qualitative debate: implications for mixed-methods research.' *Quality and Quantity 36*, 1, 43–53.

Schumacher, K. and Calvet, C. (2007) 'The 'AQR-instrument' (Assessment of the Quality of Relationship) –An Observation Instrument to Assess the Quality of a Relationship.' In T. Wosch and T. Wigram (eds) *Microanalysis in Music Therapy: Methods, Techniques and Applications for Clinicians, Researchers, Educators and Students.* London: Jessica Kingsley Publishers.

Sera, Y. and Beaudry, S. (2007) *Monitoring & Evaluation.* Available at http://siteresources.worldbank.org/INTBELARUS/Resources/M&E.pdf, accessed on 5 April 2013.

Simpson, P.F., French, R. and Harvey, C.E. (2002) 'Leadership and negative capability.' *Human Relations 55*, 10, 1209–1226.

Smeijsters, H. and Aasgaard, T. (2005) 'Qualitative Case Study Research.' In B. Wheeler (ed.) *Music Therapy Research.* Gilsum, NH: Barcelona Publishers.

Smith, J. and Osborn, M. (2003) 'Interpretative Phenomenological Analysis.' In J. Smith (ed.) *Qualitative Psychology: A Practical Guide to Research Methods.* London: Sage.

Smith, T. (2003) *An Evaluation of Sorts: Learning from Common Knowledge.* Durham: CAHHM, University of Durham.

Starks, H. and Trinidad, S. (2007) 'Choose your method: a comparison of phenomenology, discourse analysis, and grounded theory.' *Qualitative Health Research 17*, 10, 1372–1380.

Stige, B. (2005) 'Participatory Action Research.' In B. Wheeler (ed.) *Music Therapy Research* (2nd Edition). Gilsum, NH: Barcelona Publishers.

The UK Copyright Service (2009) *Fact sheet P-01: UK Copyright Law.* Available at www.copyrightservice.co.uk/copyright/p01_uk_copyright_law, accessed on 10 October 2013.

Tsiris, G. and Hartley, N. (2013) 'Research and Evaluation.' In N. Hartley (ed.) *End of Life Care: A Guide for Therapists, Artists and Arts Therapists.* London: Jessica Kingsley Publishers.

United Nations Development Programme (2009) *Handbook on Planning, Monitoring and Evaluating for Development Results.* Available at http://web.undp.org/evaluation/handbook/documents/english/pme-handbook.pdf, accessed on 9 September 2013.

United Nations World Food Programme (undated) *Monitoring & Evaluation Guidelines: What is RBM Oriented M&E.* Available at http://home.wfp.org/stellent/groups/public/documents/ko/mekb_module_7.pdf, accessed on 5 April 2013.

Wade, D. (2005) 'Ethics, audit, and research: all shades of grey.' *British Medical Journal 330*, 7489, 468–471.

Wadsworth, Y. (2011) *Everyday Evaluation on the Run: The User-Friendly Introductory Guide to Effective Evaluation.* Walnut Creek, CA: Left Coast Press.

Westhues, A., Ochocka, J., Jacobson, N., Simich, L. *et al.* (2008) 'Developing theory from complexity: reflections on a collaborative mixed method participatory action research study.' *Qualitative Health Research 18*, 5, 701–717.

White, M. (2009) *Arts Development in Community Health: A Social Tonic.* Oxford: Radcliffe.

# Index